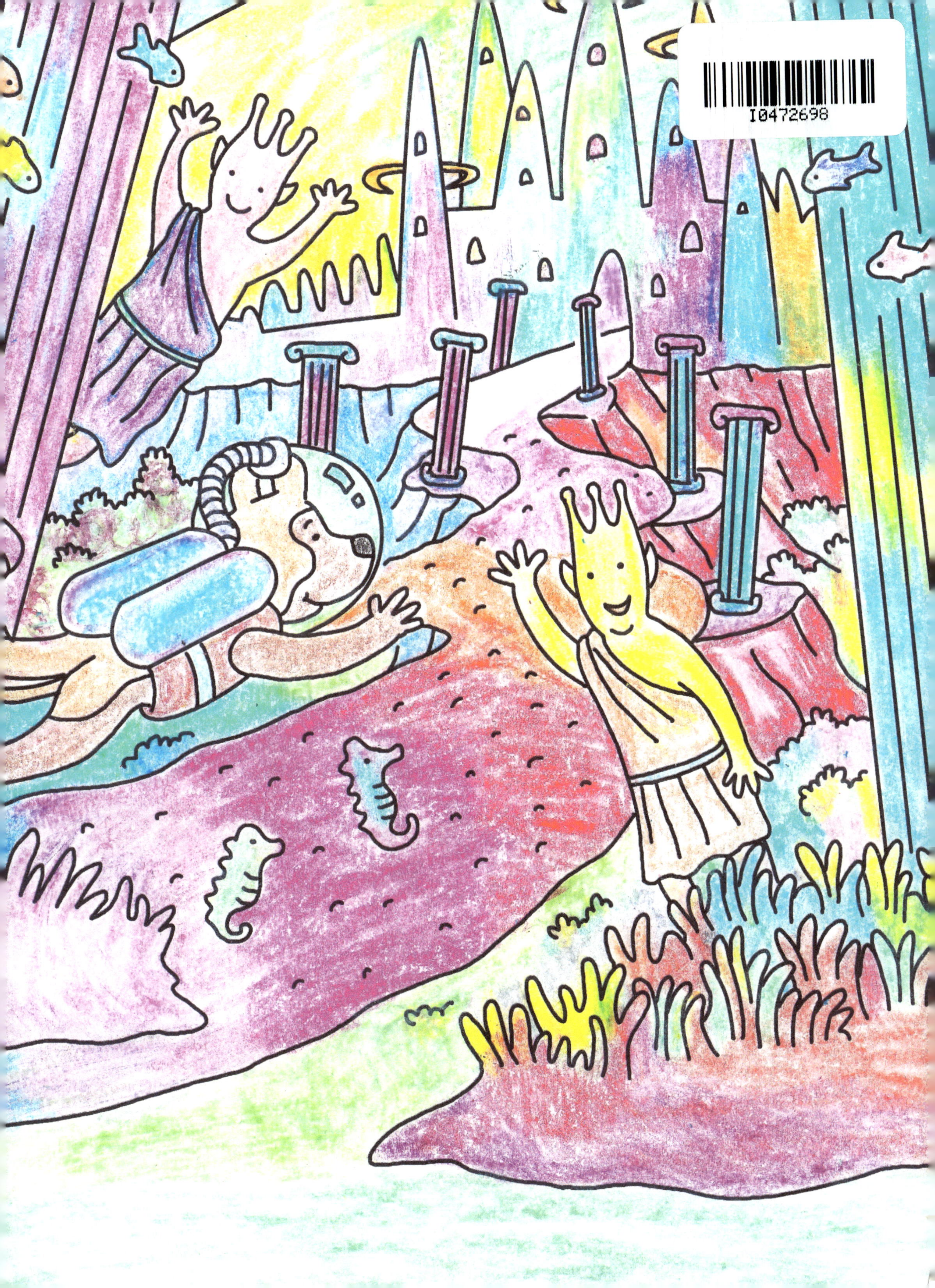

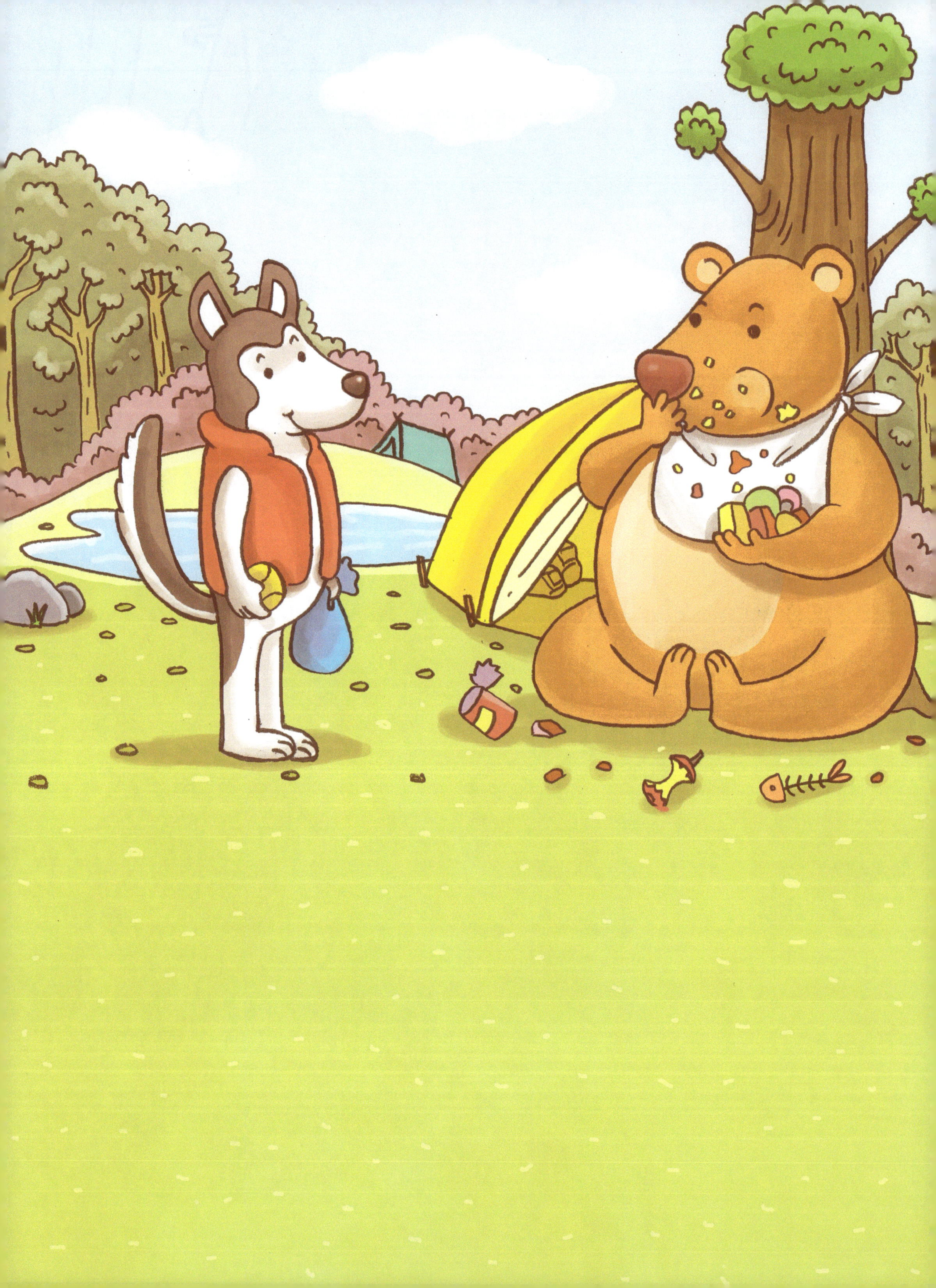

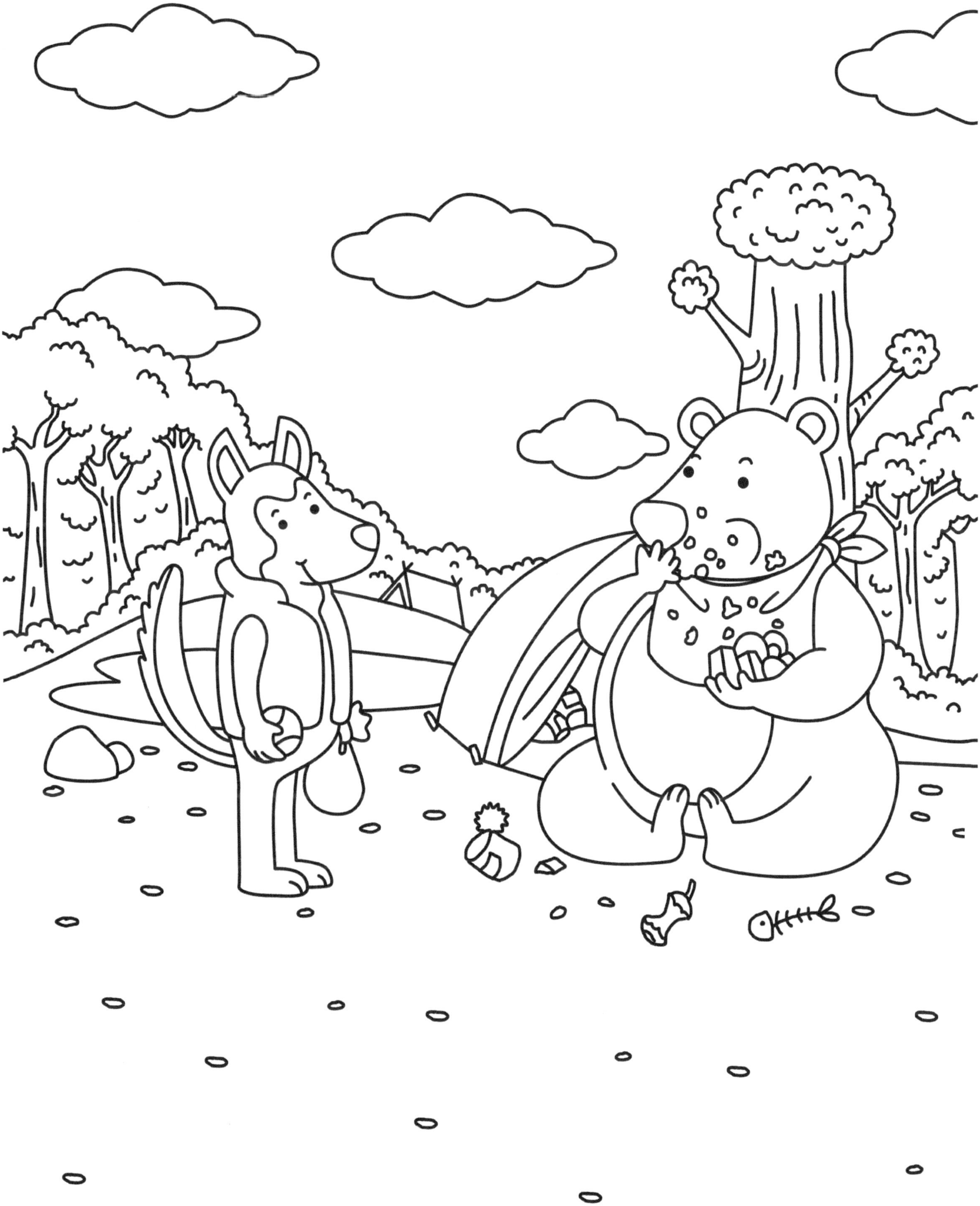

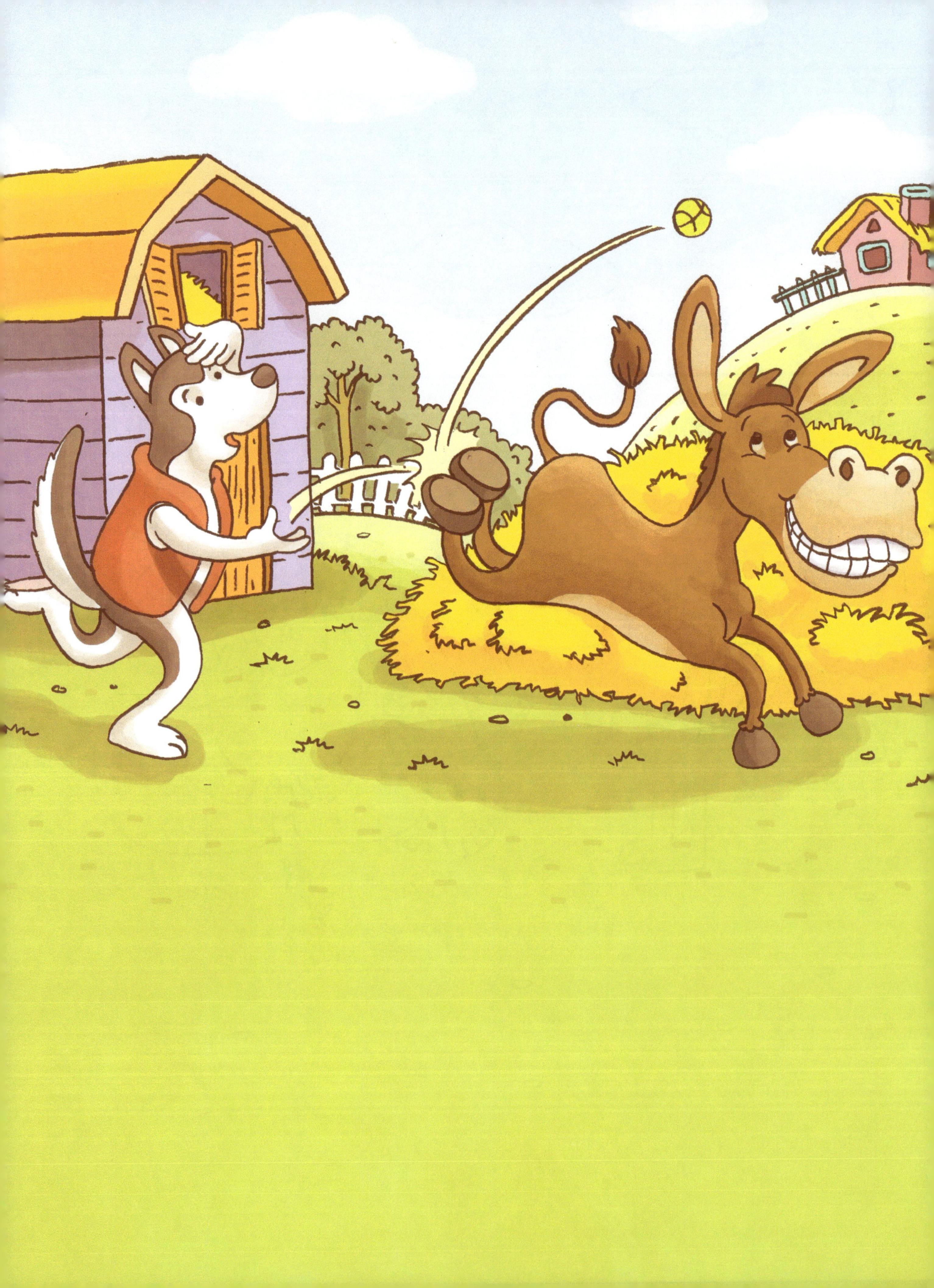

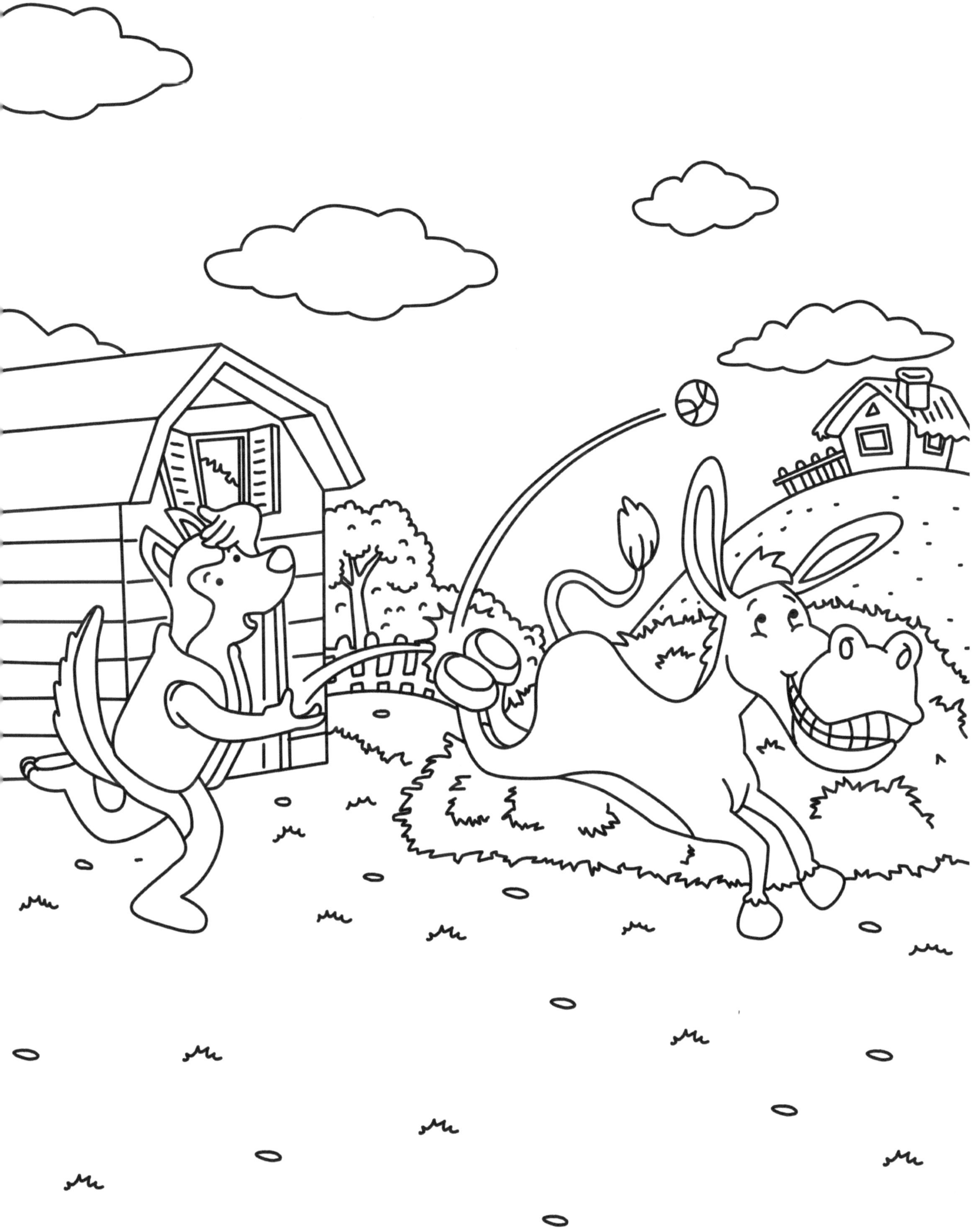

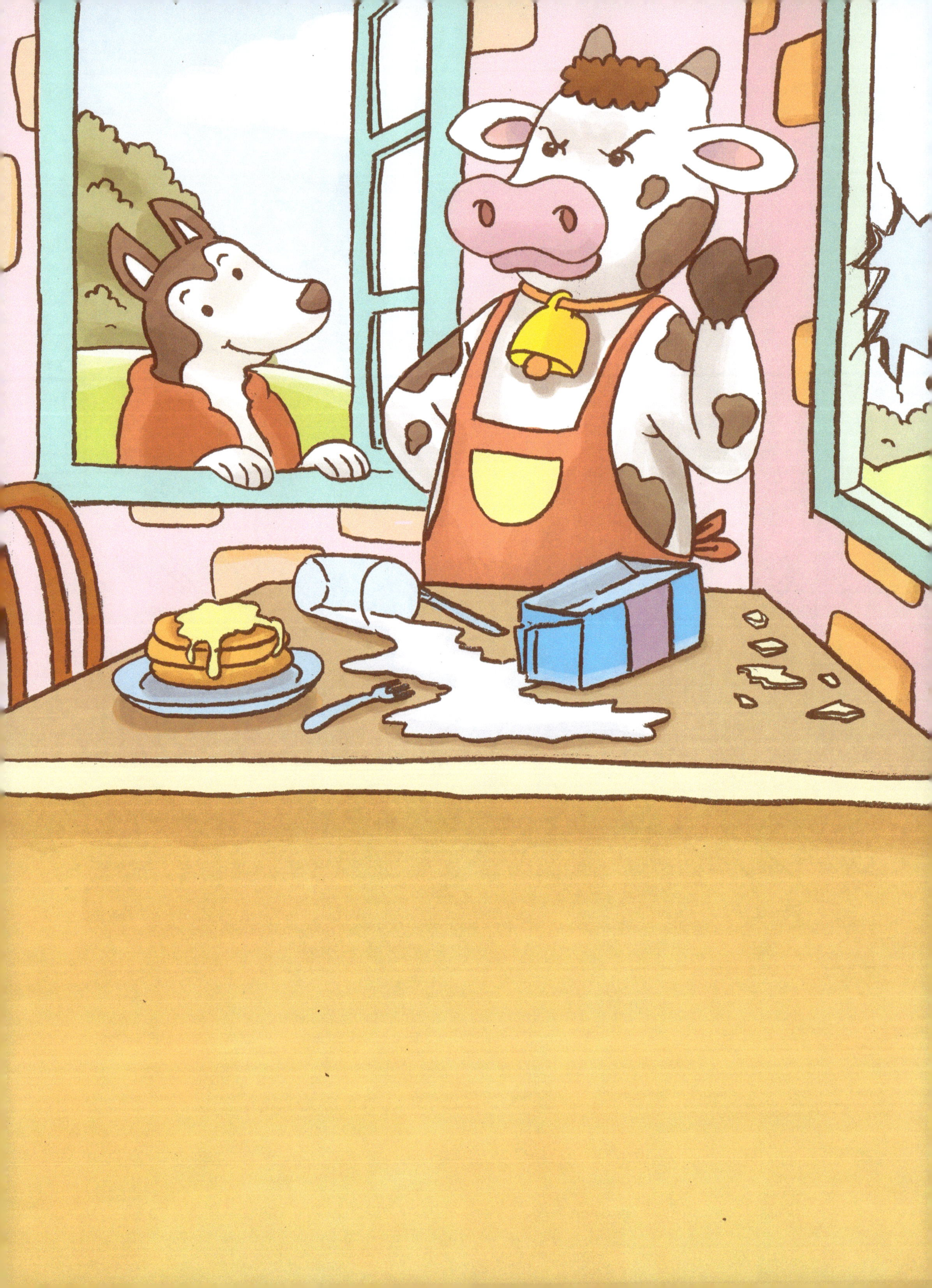

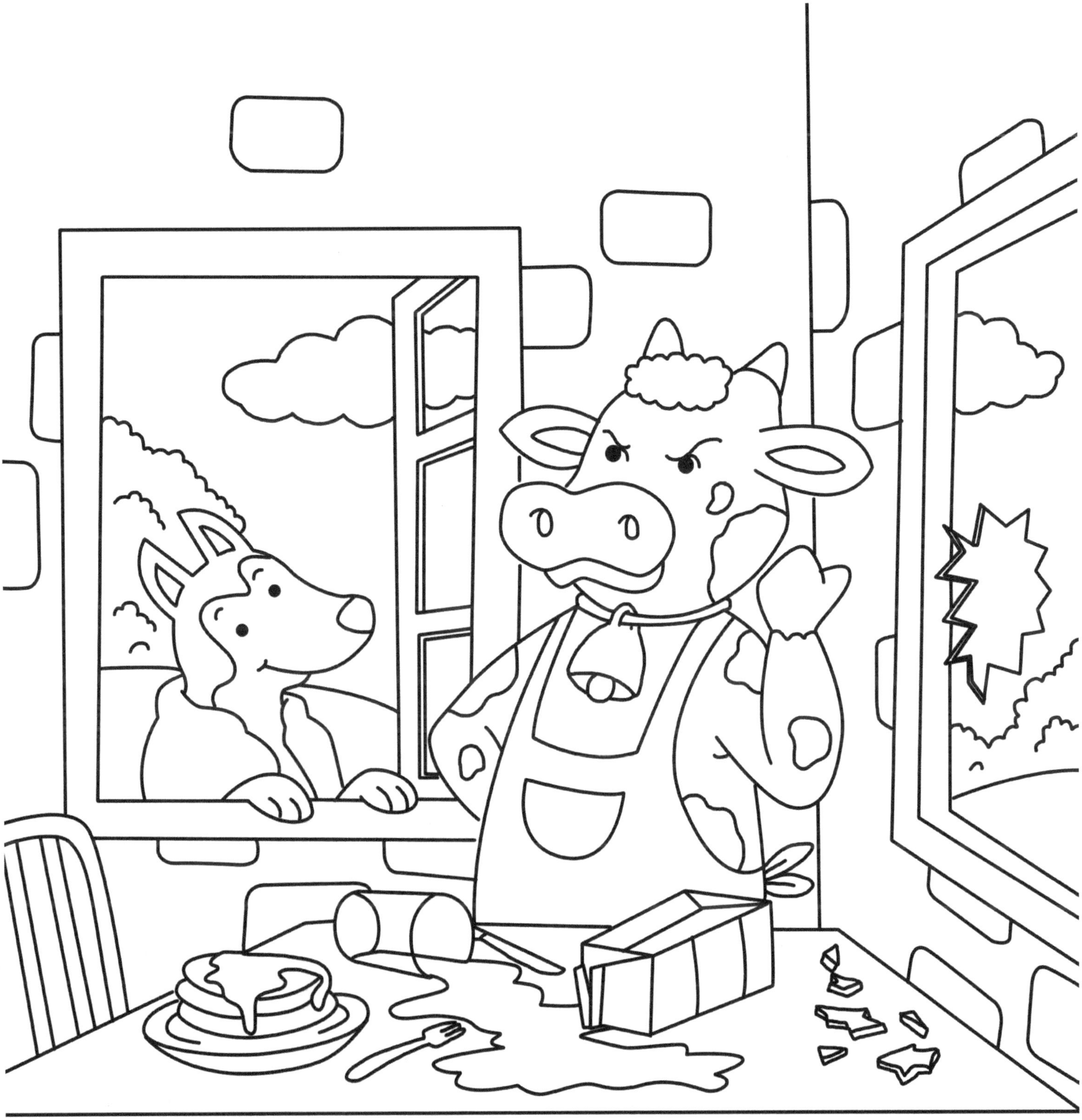

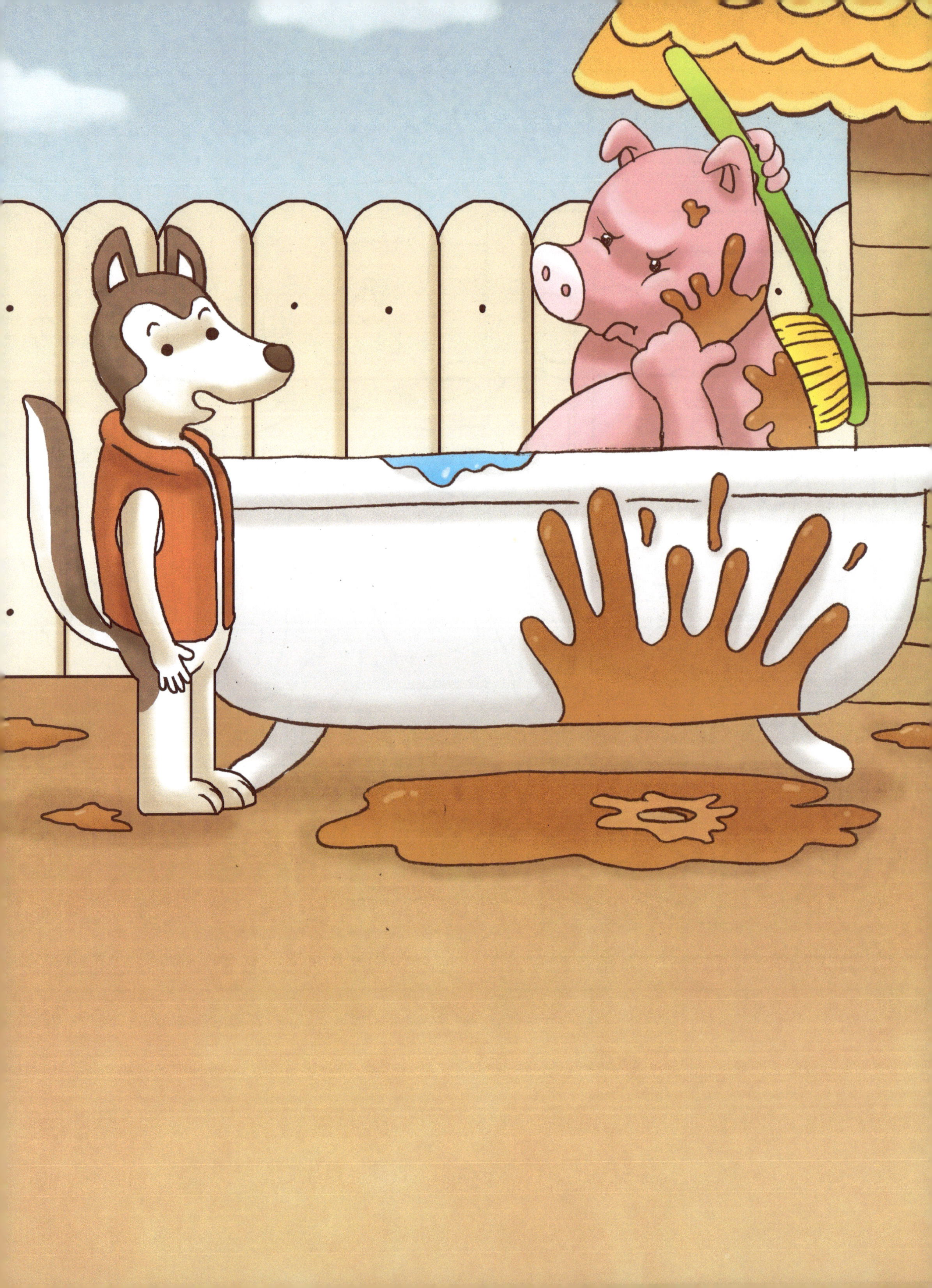

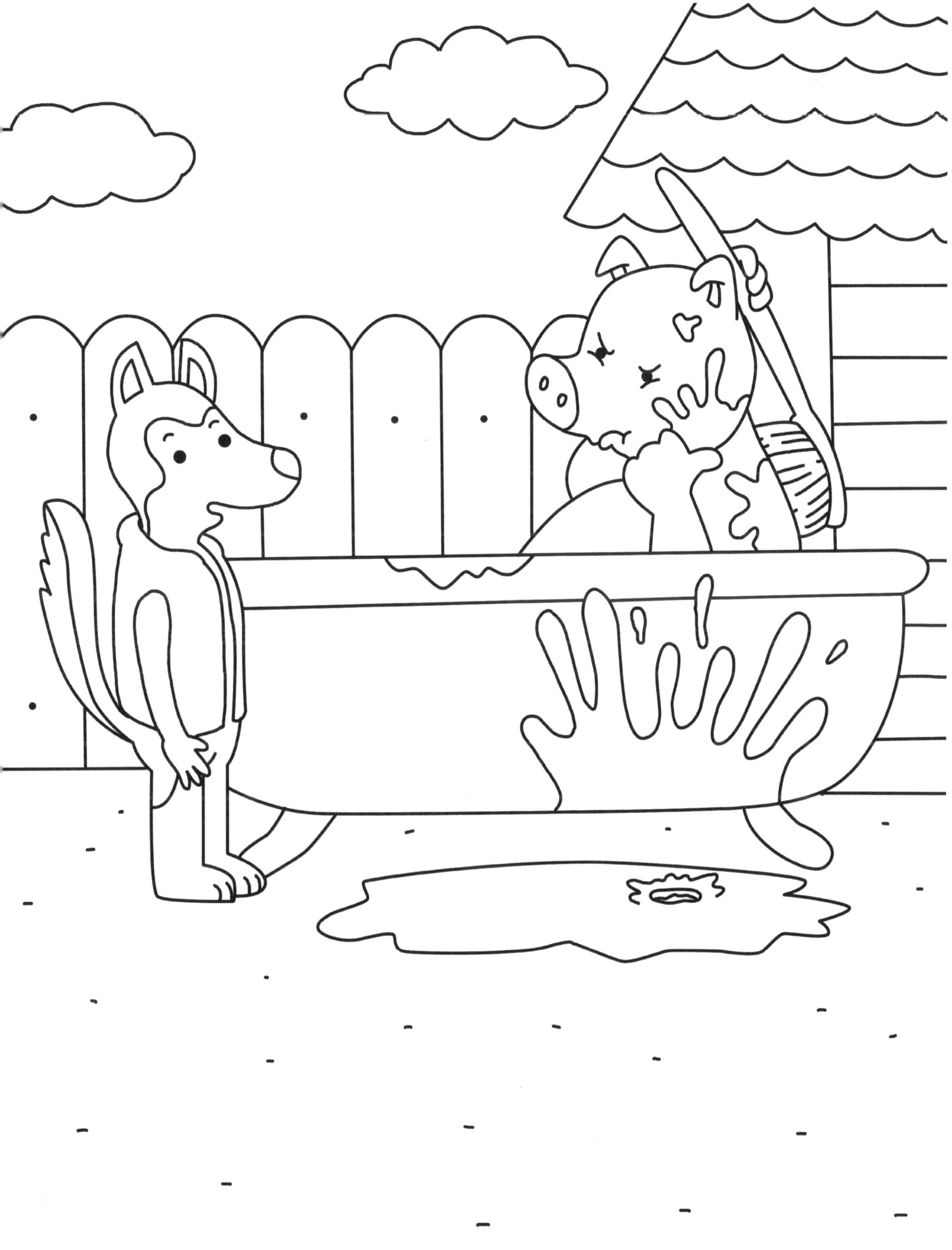

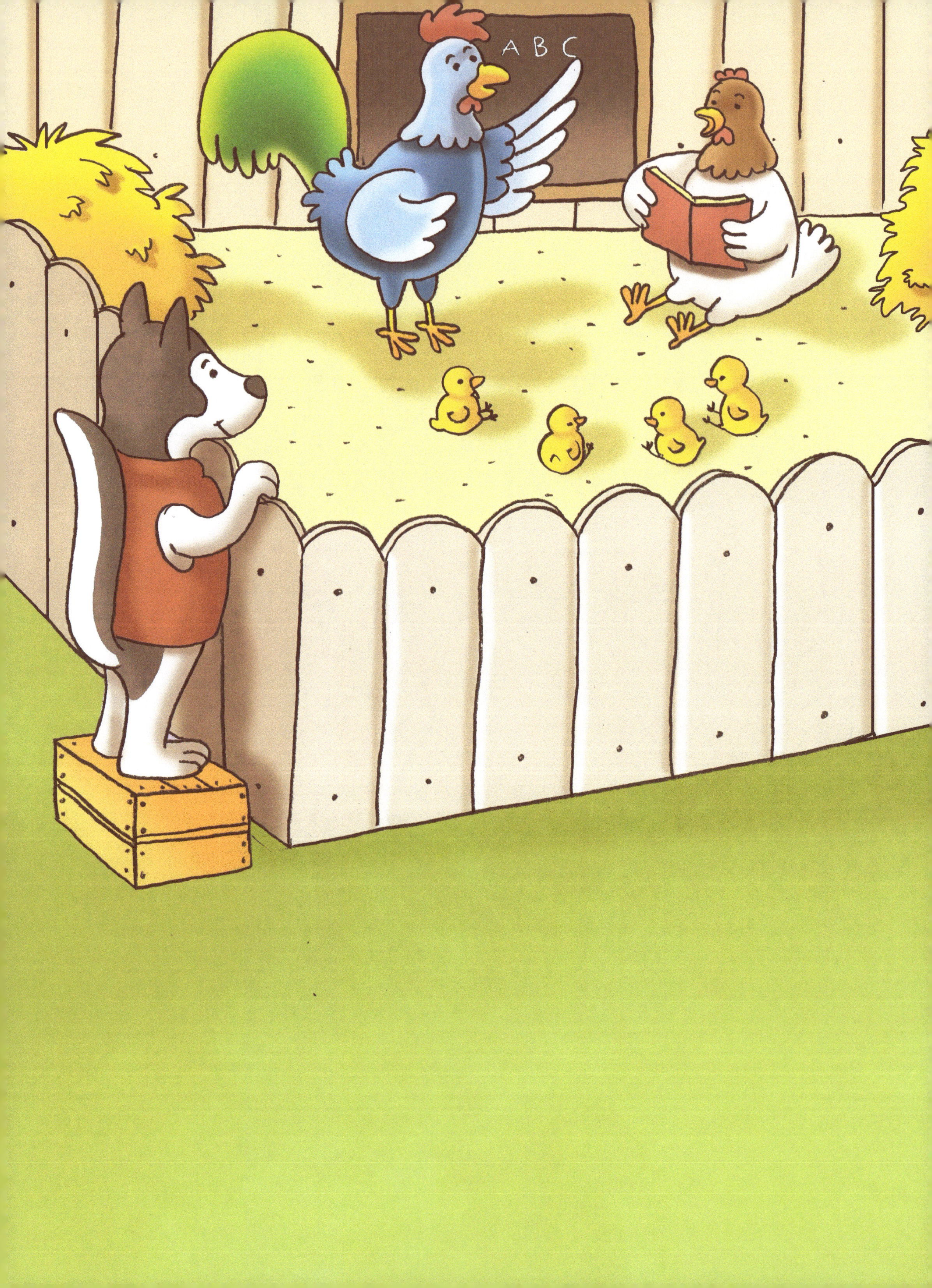
A B C

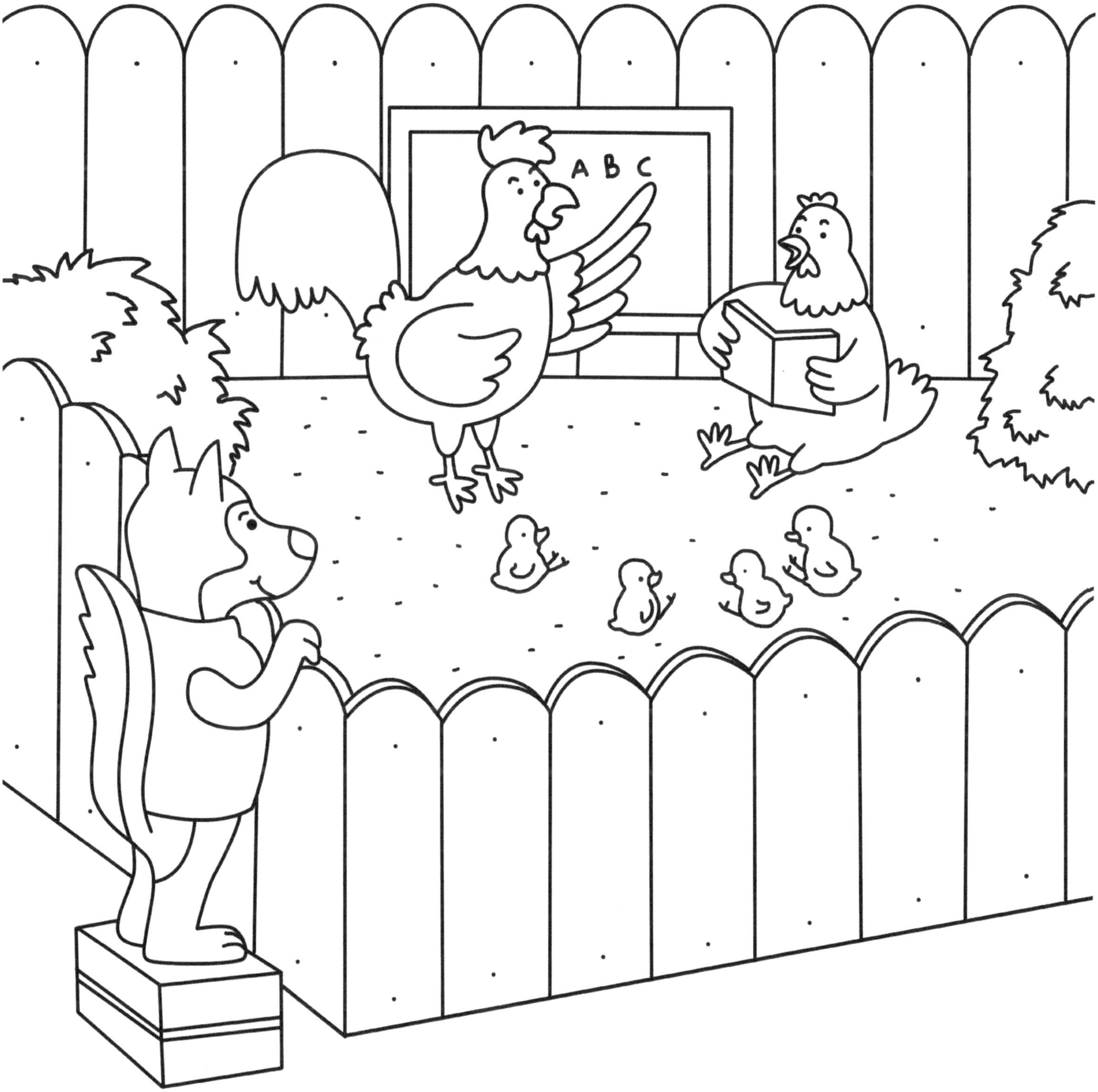
A B C

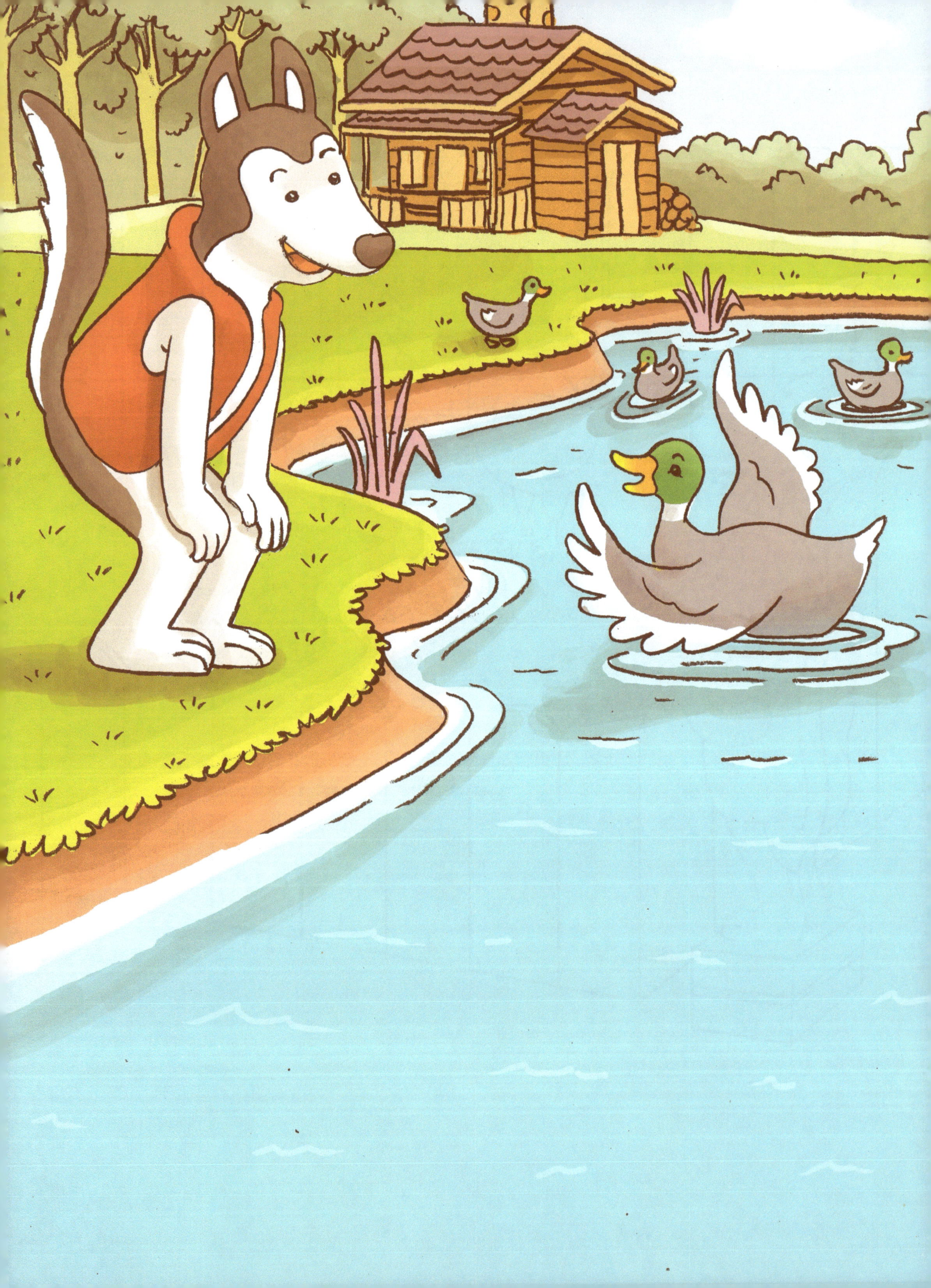

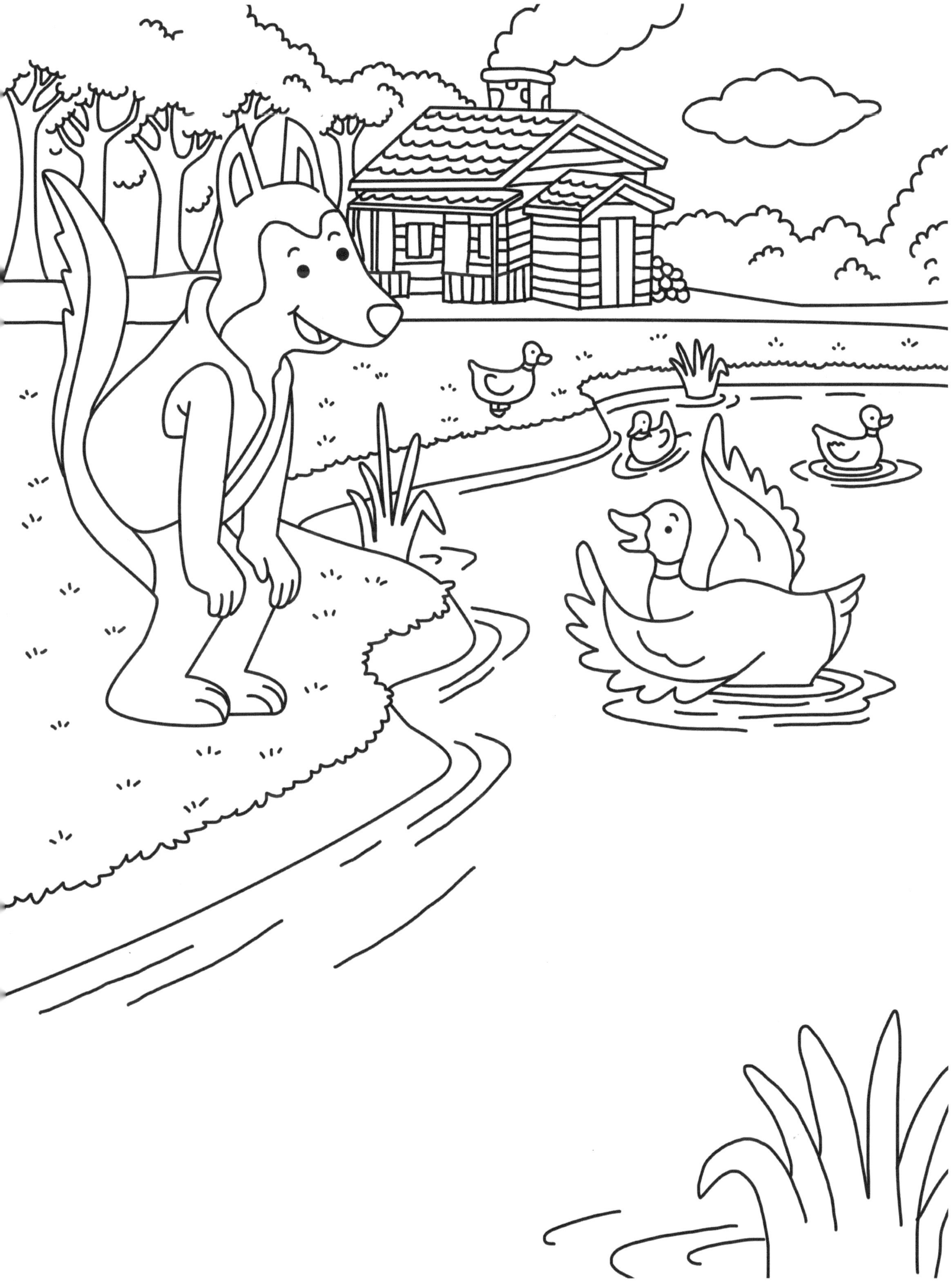

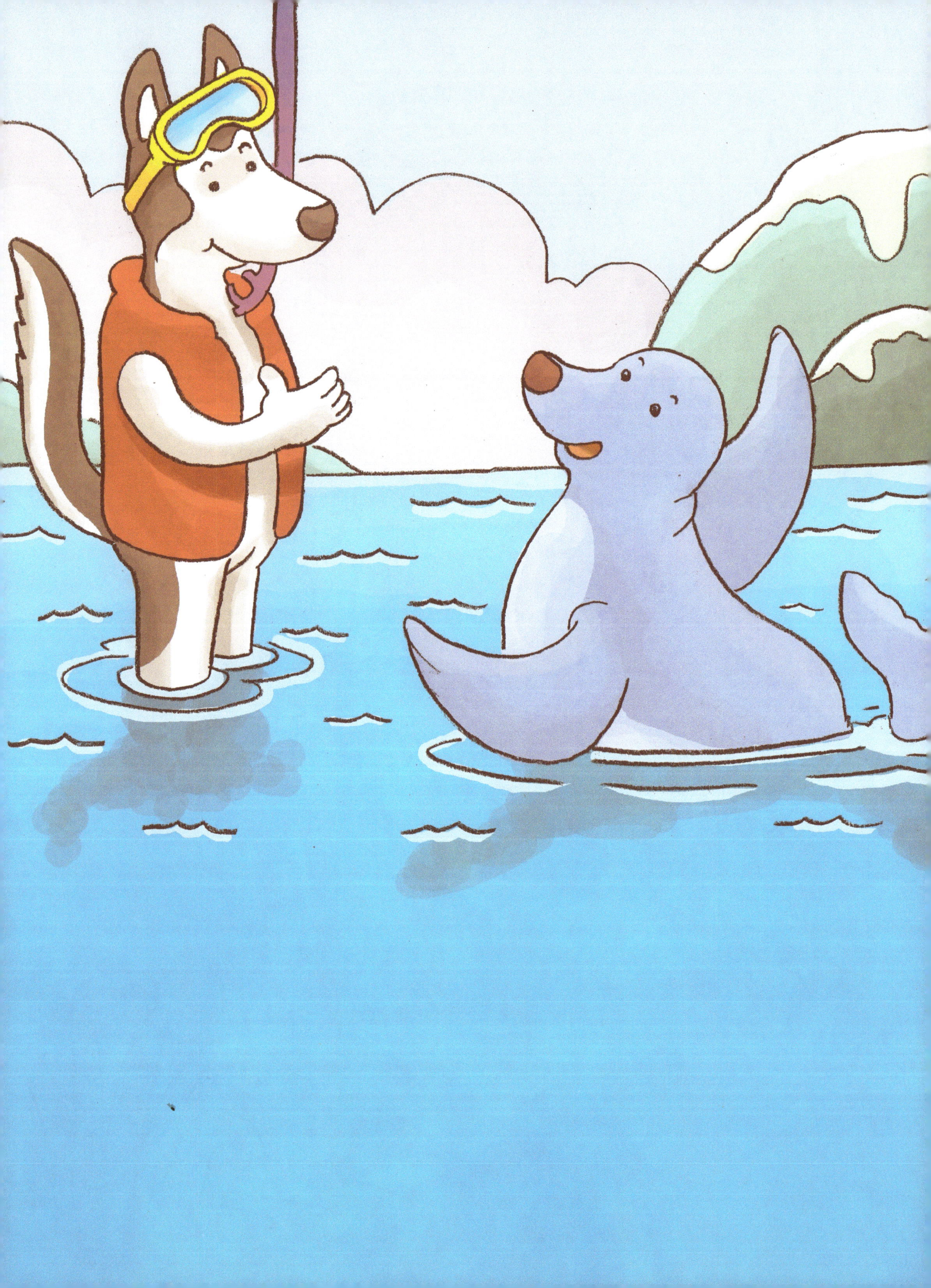

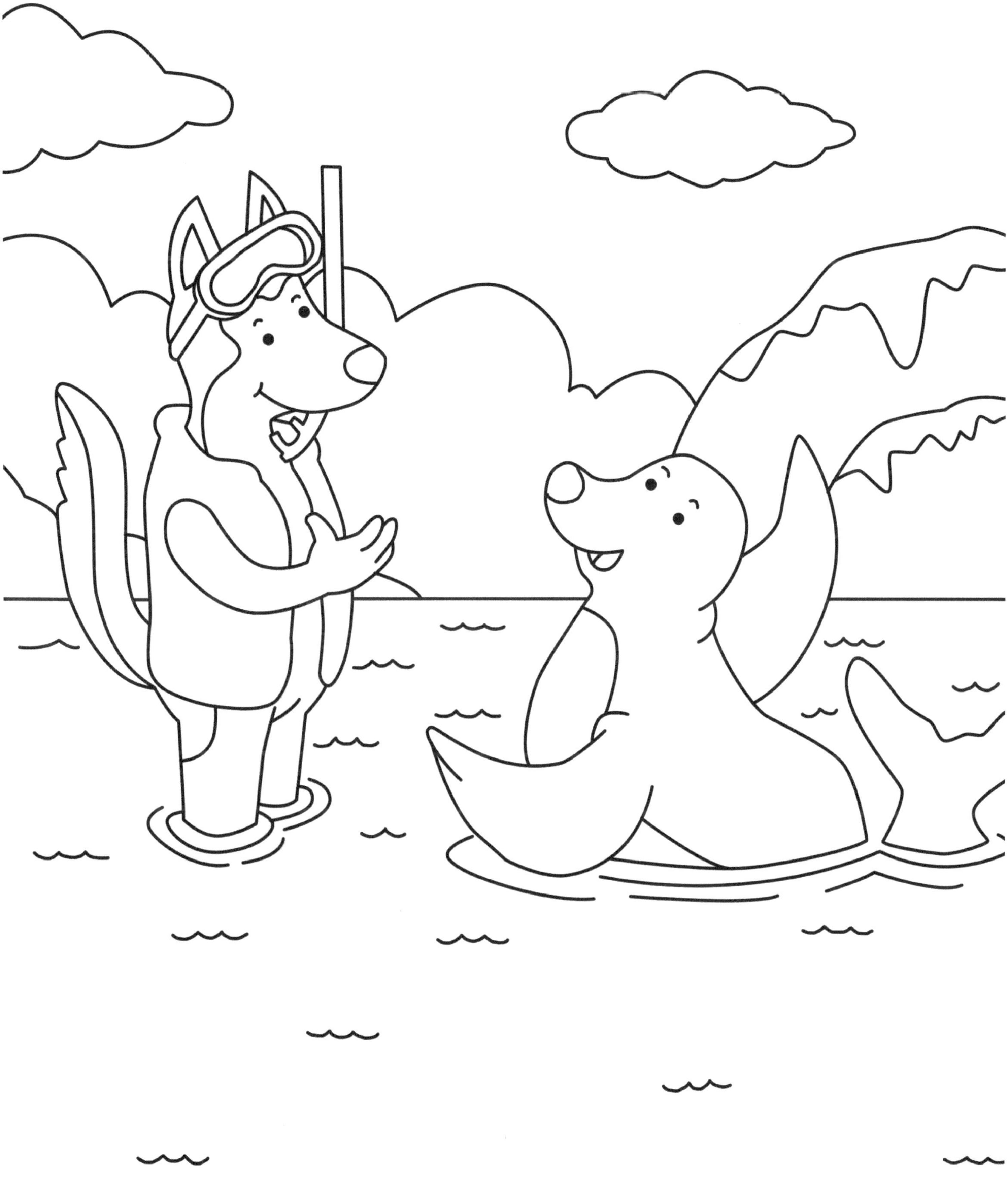

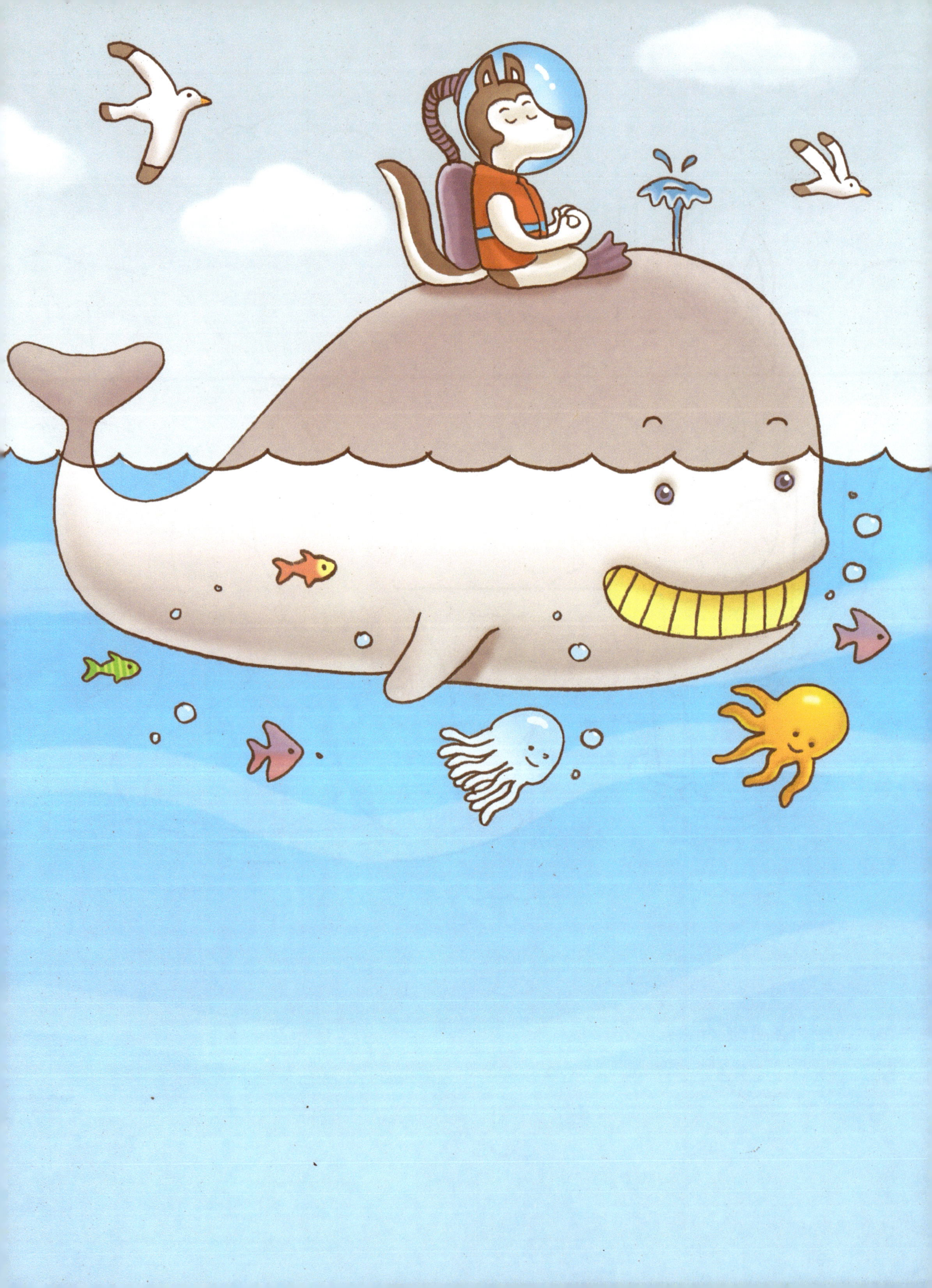

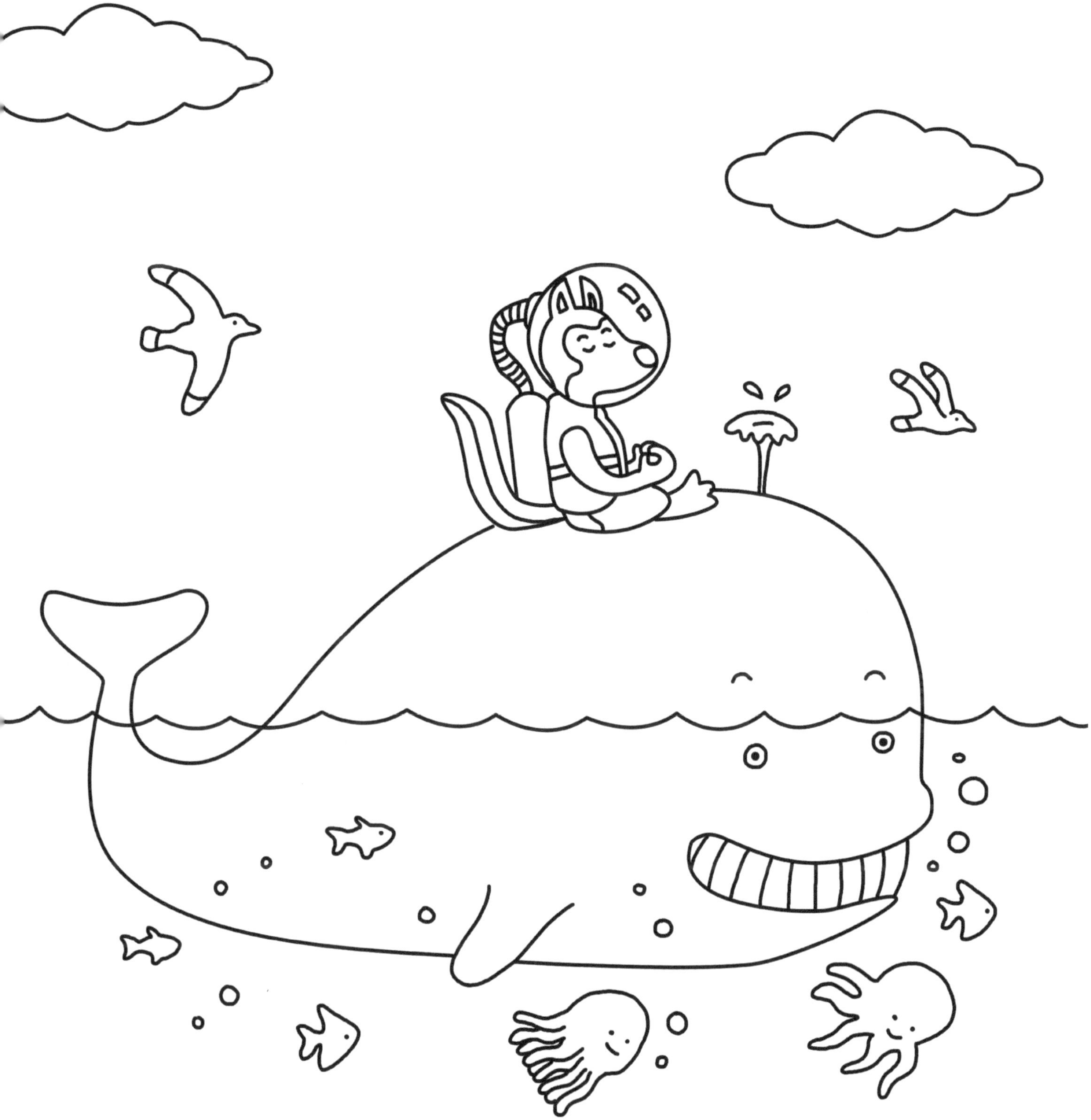

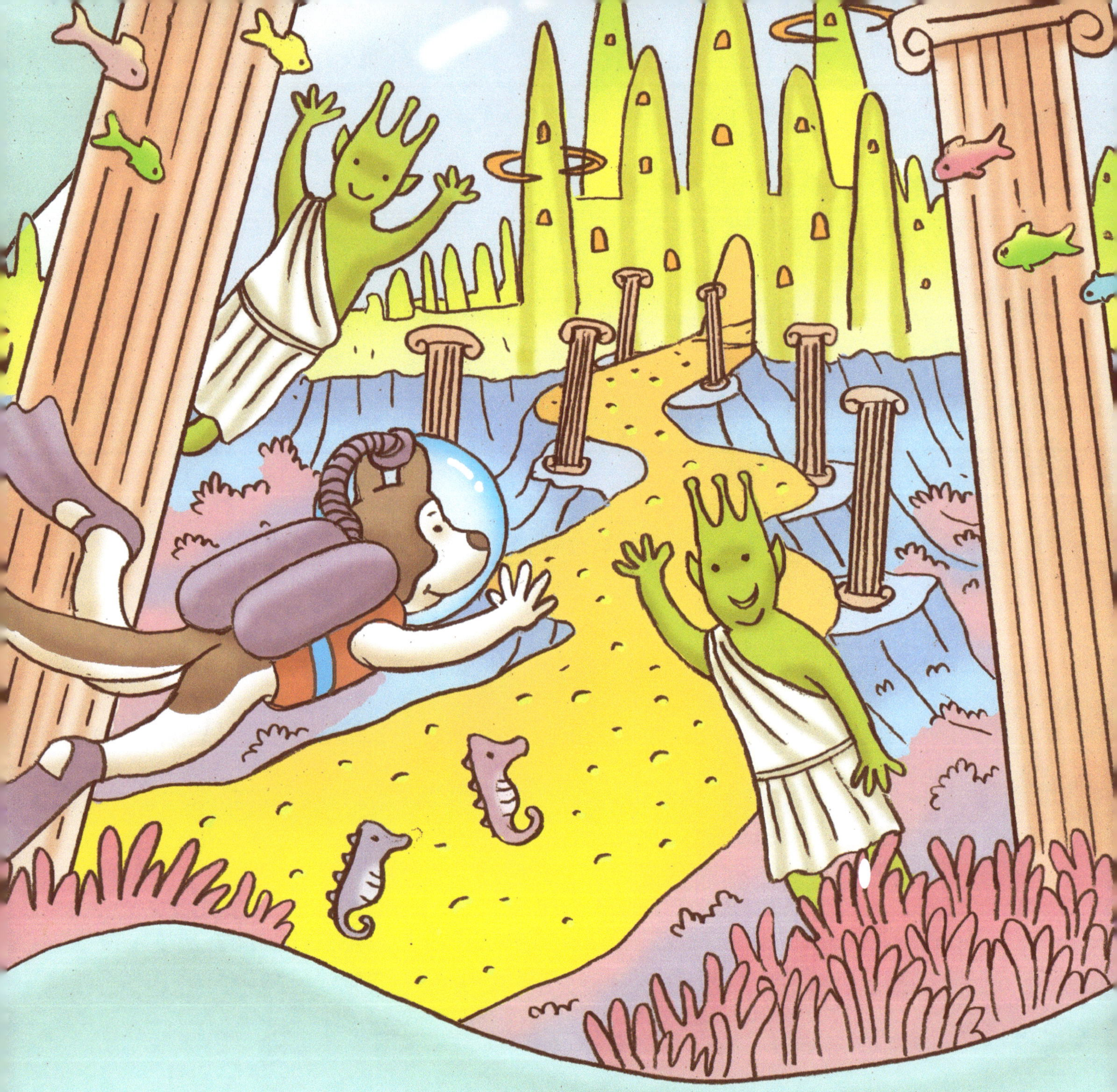

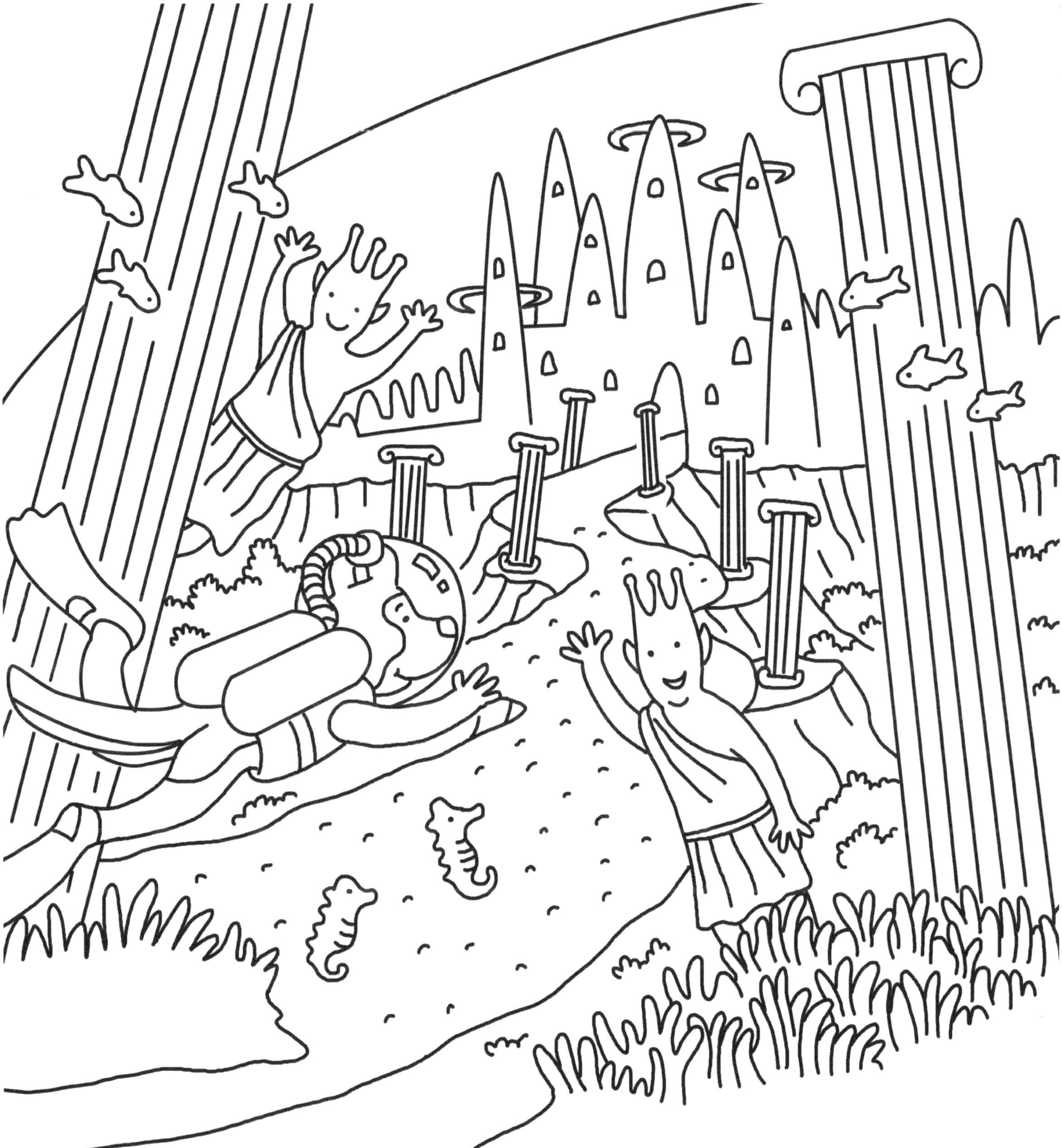

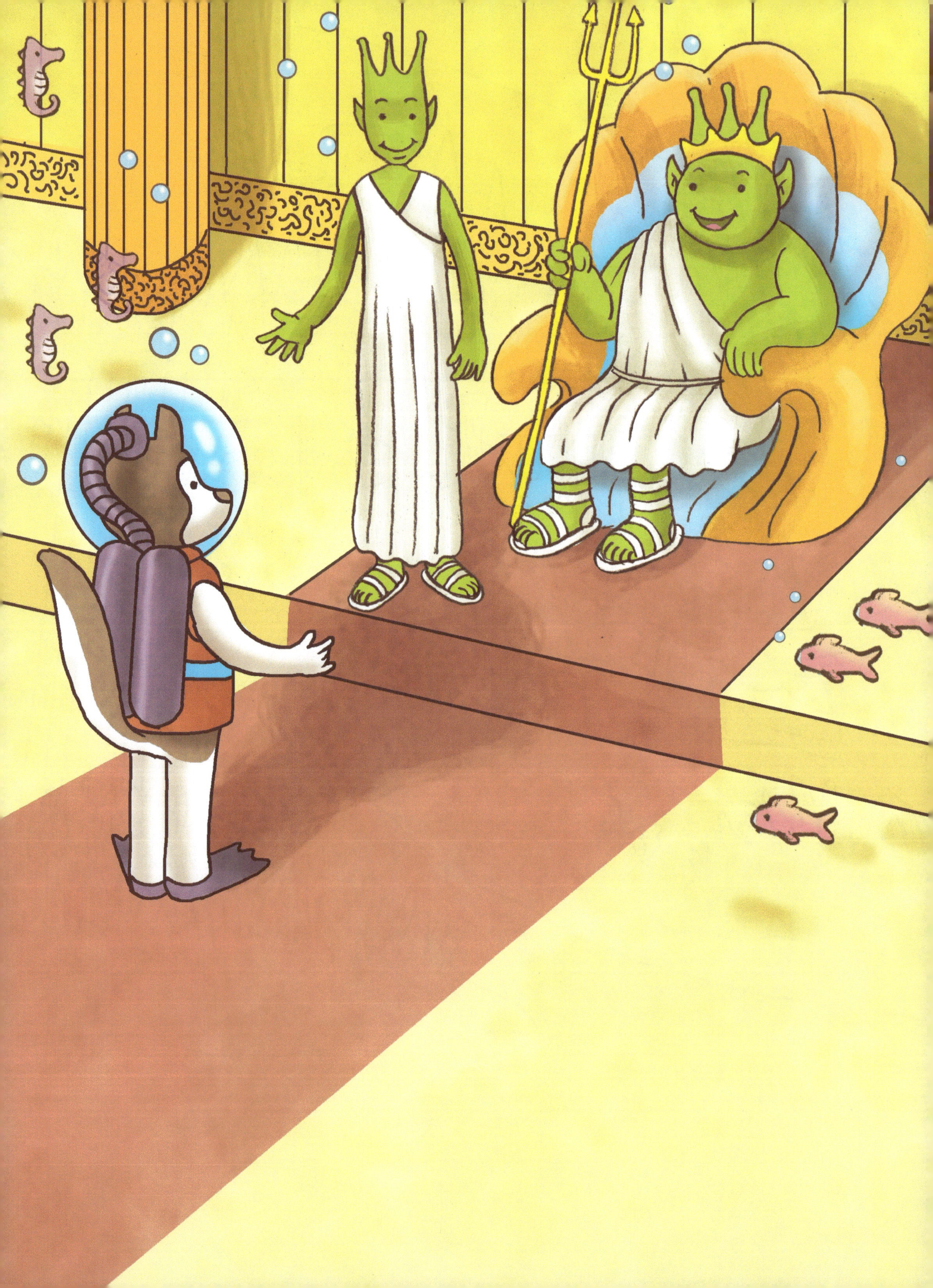

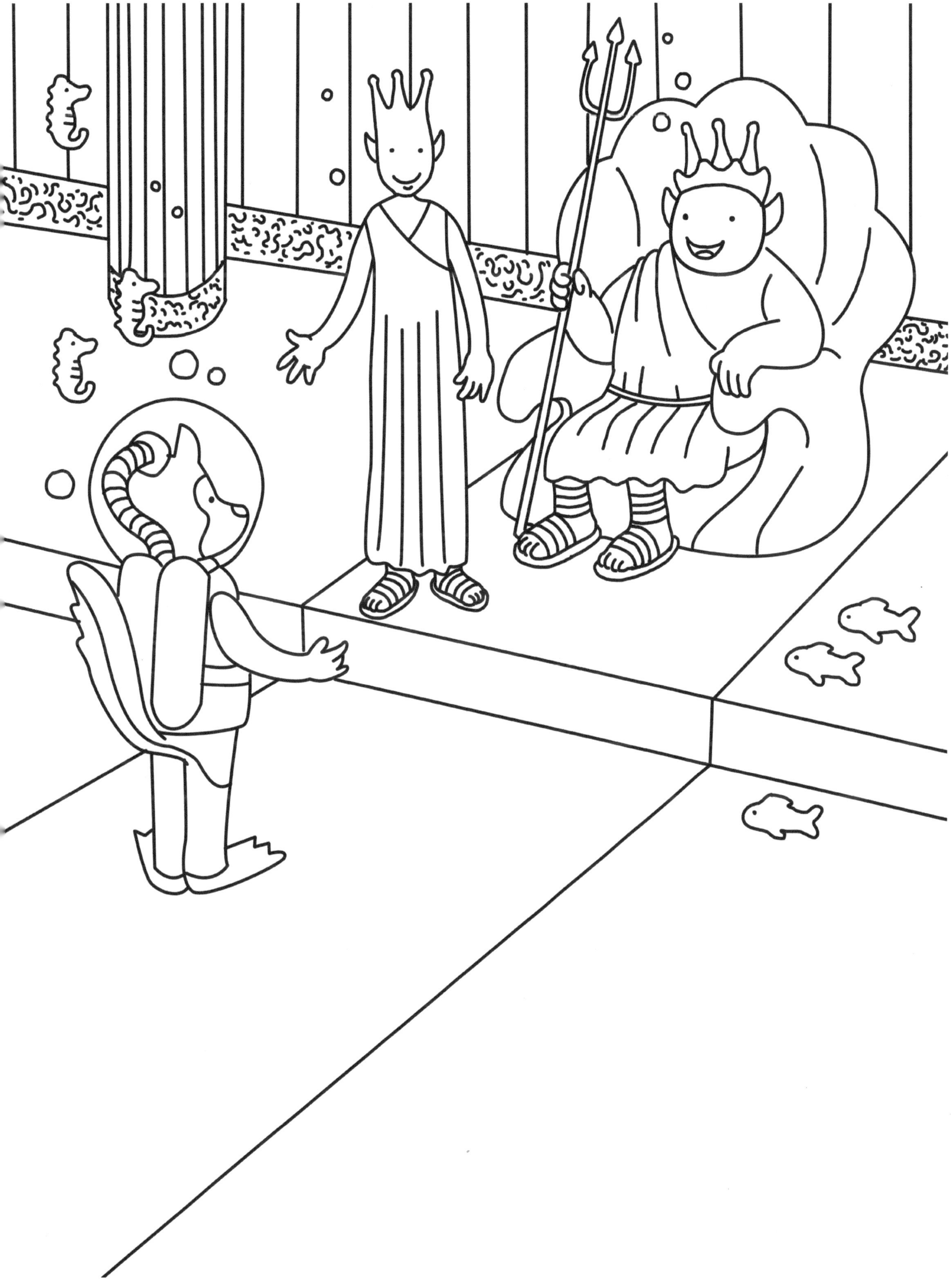

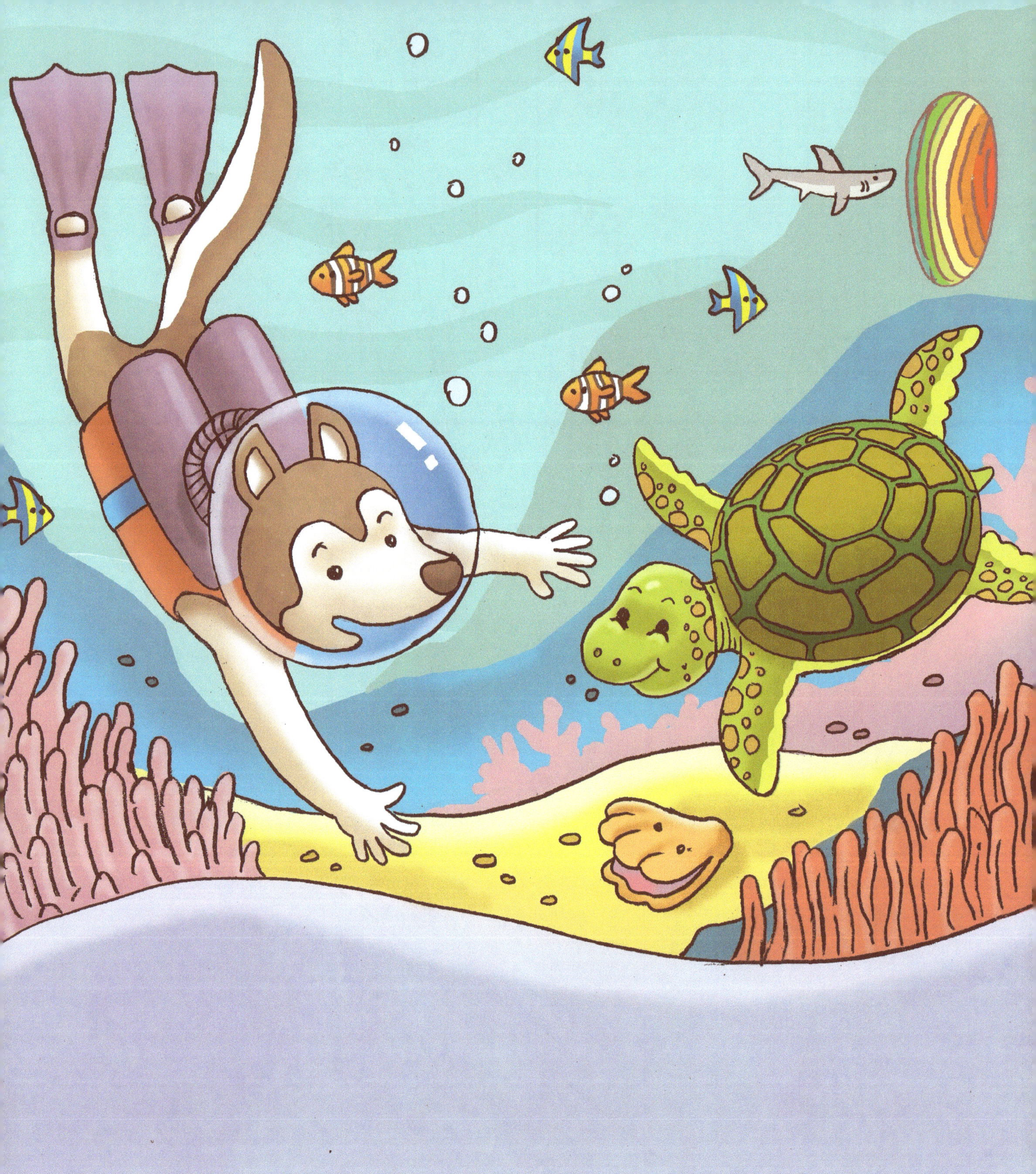

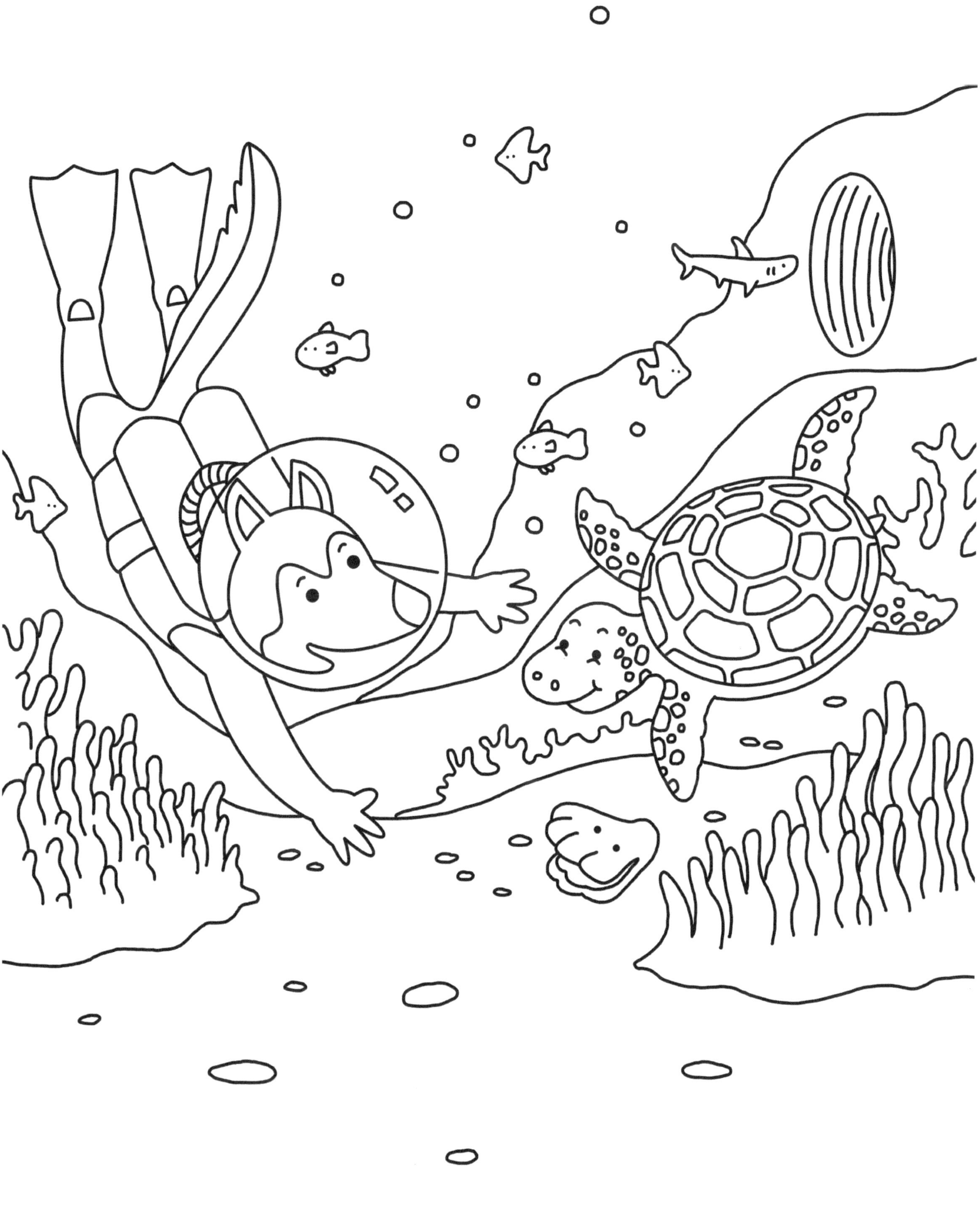

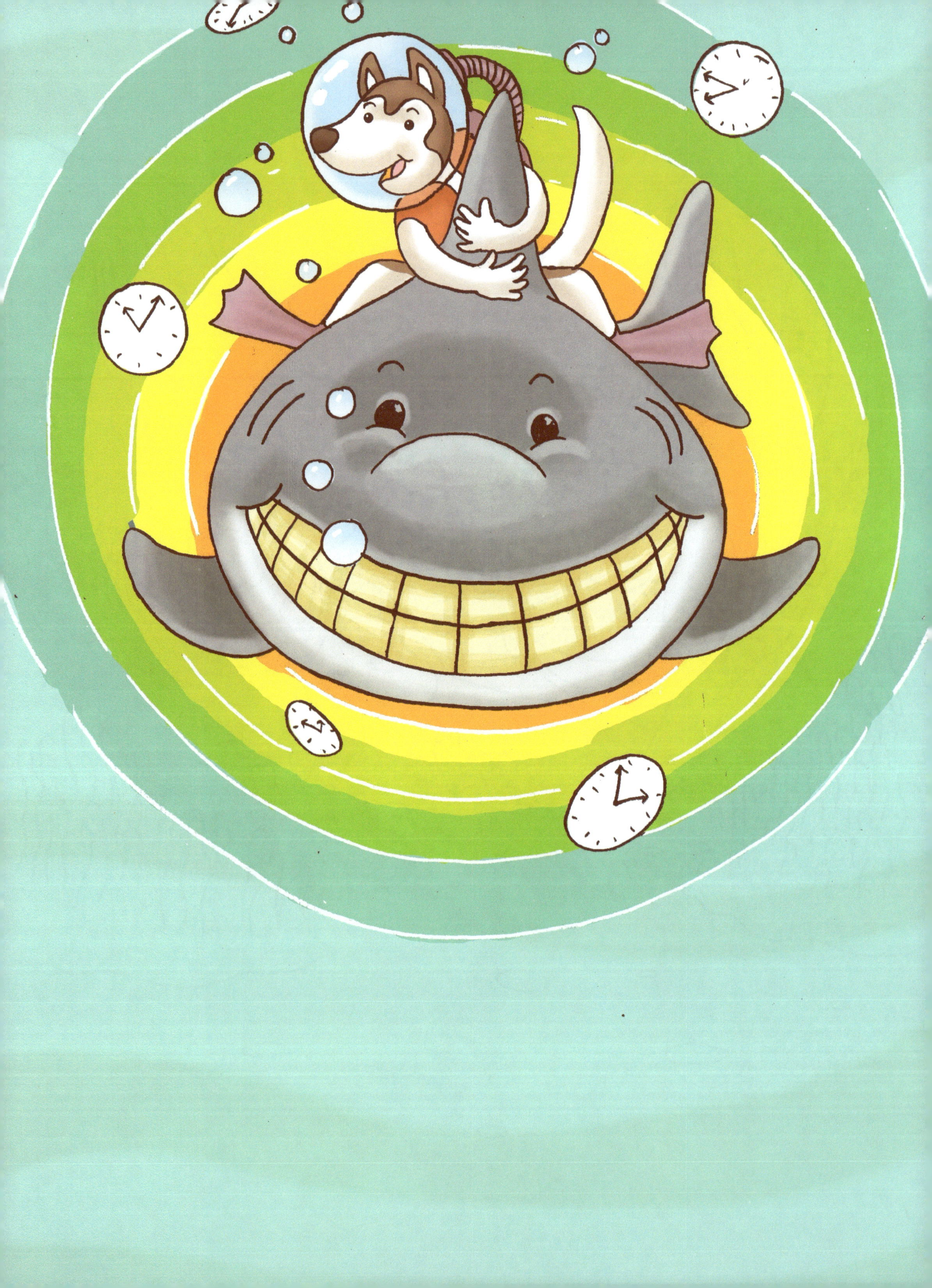

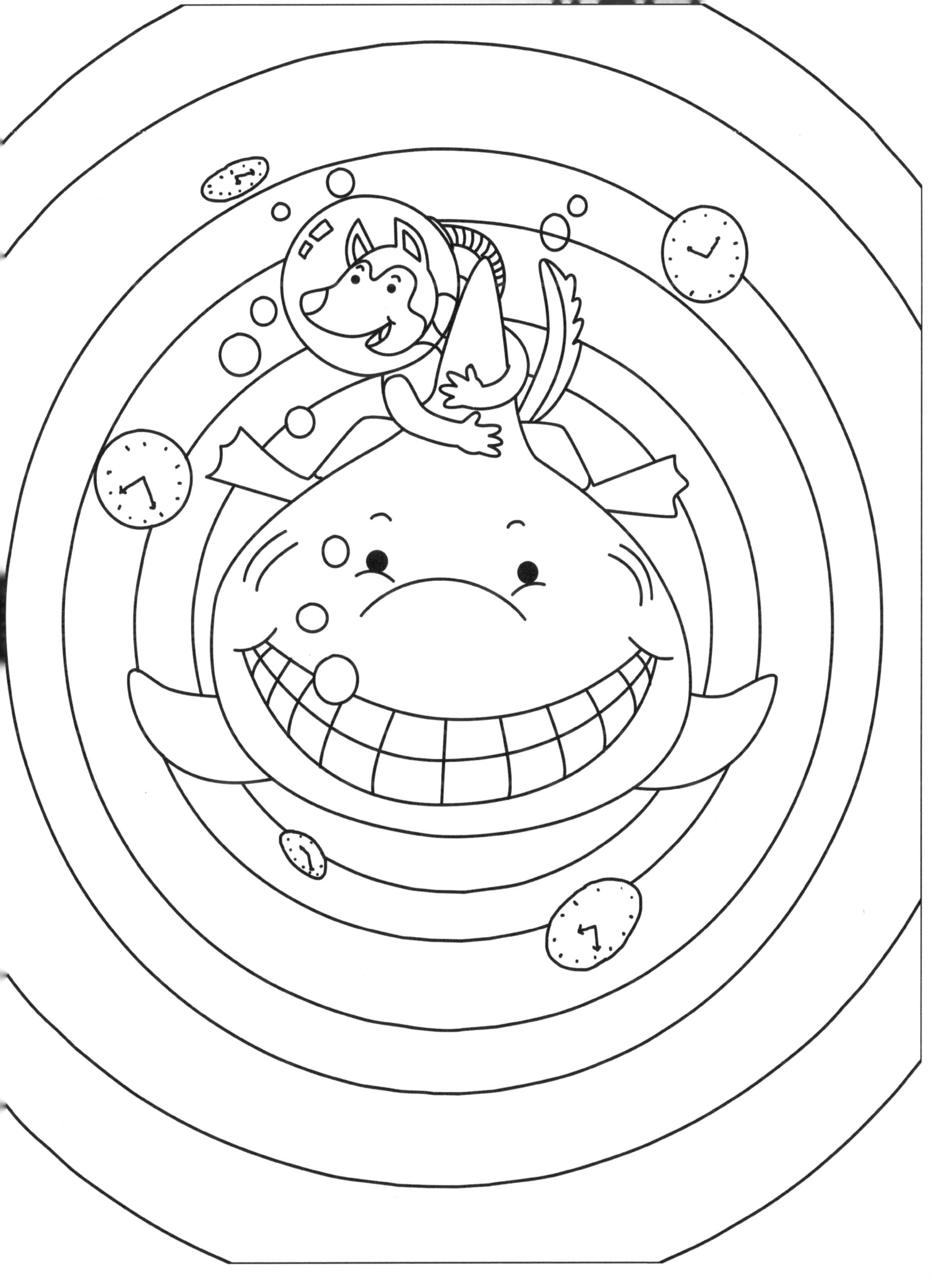

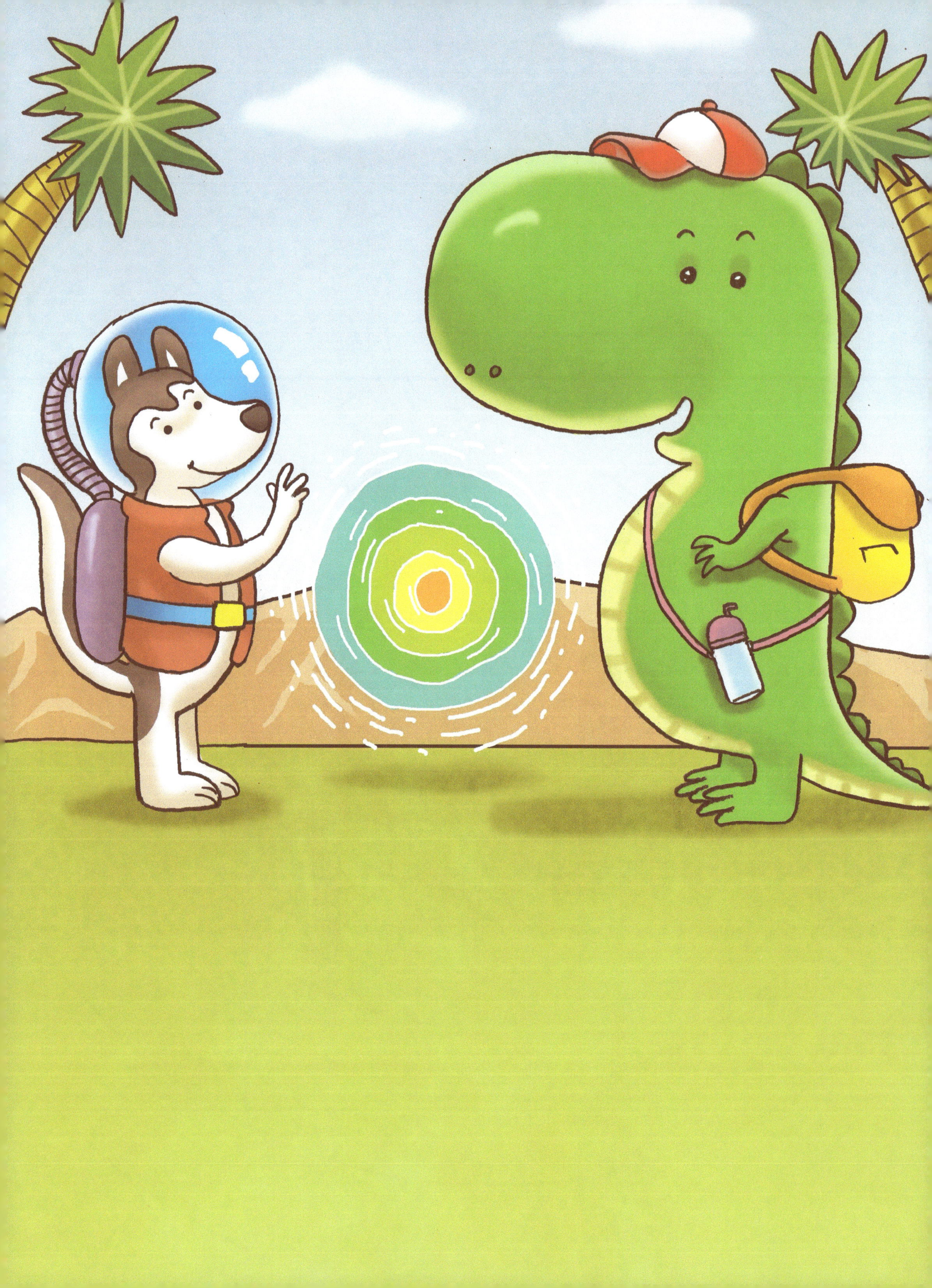

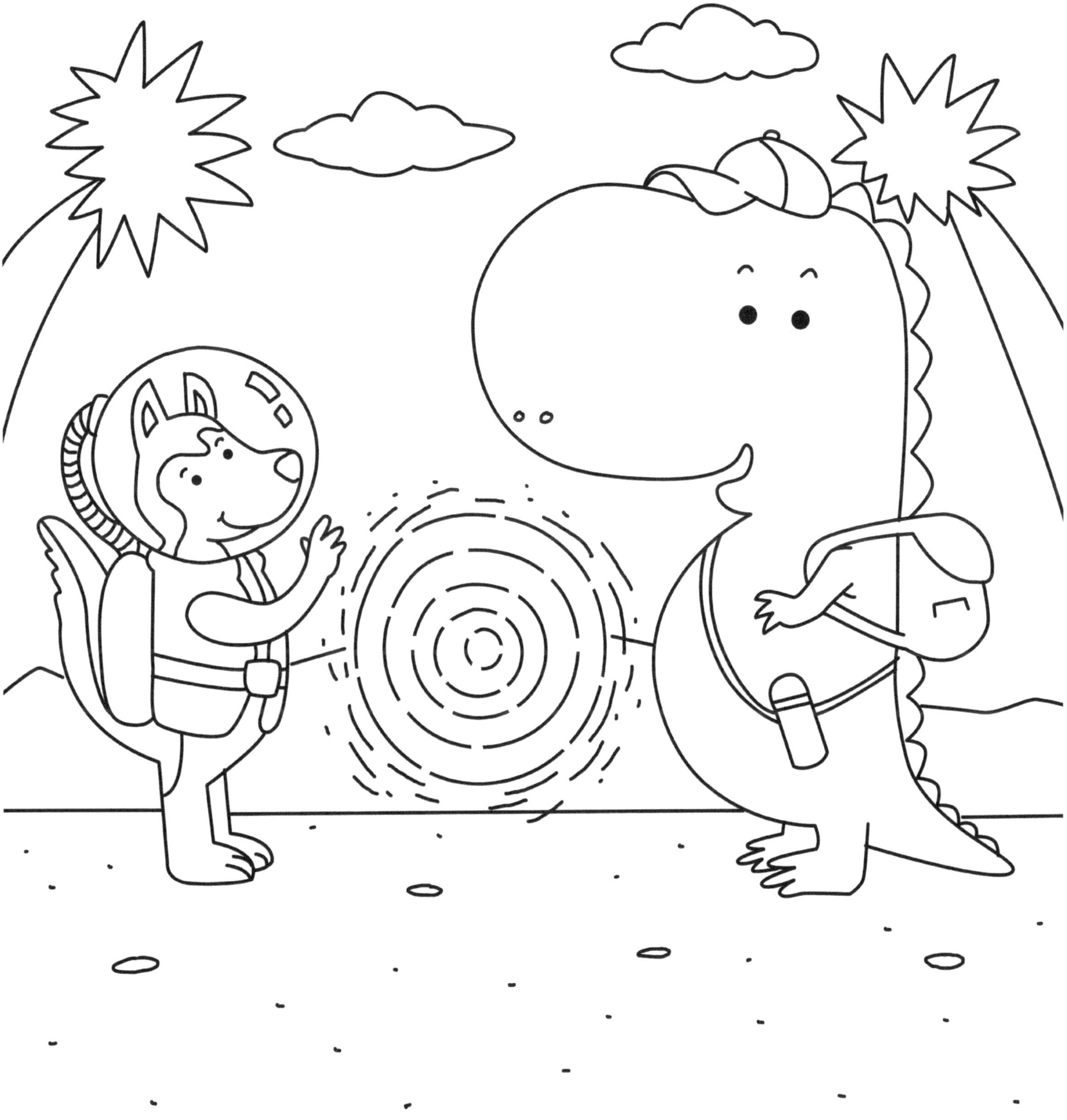

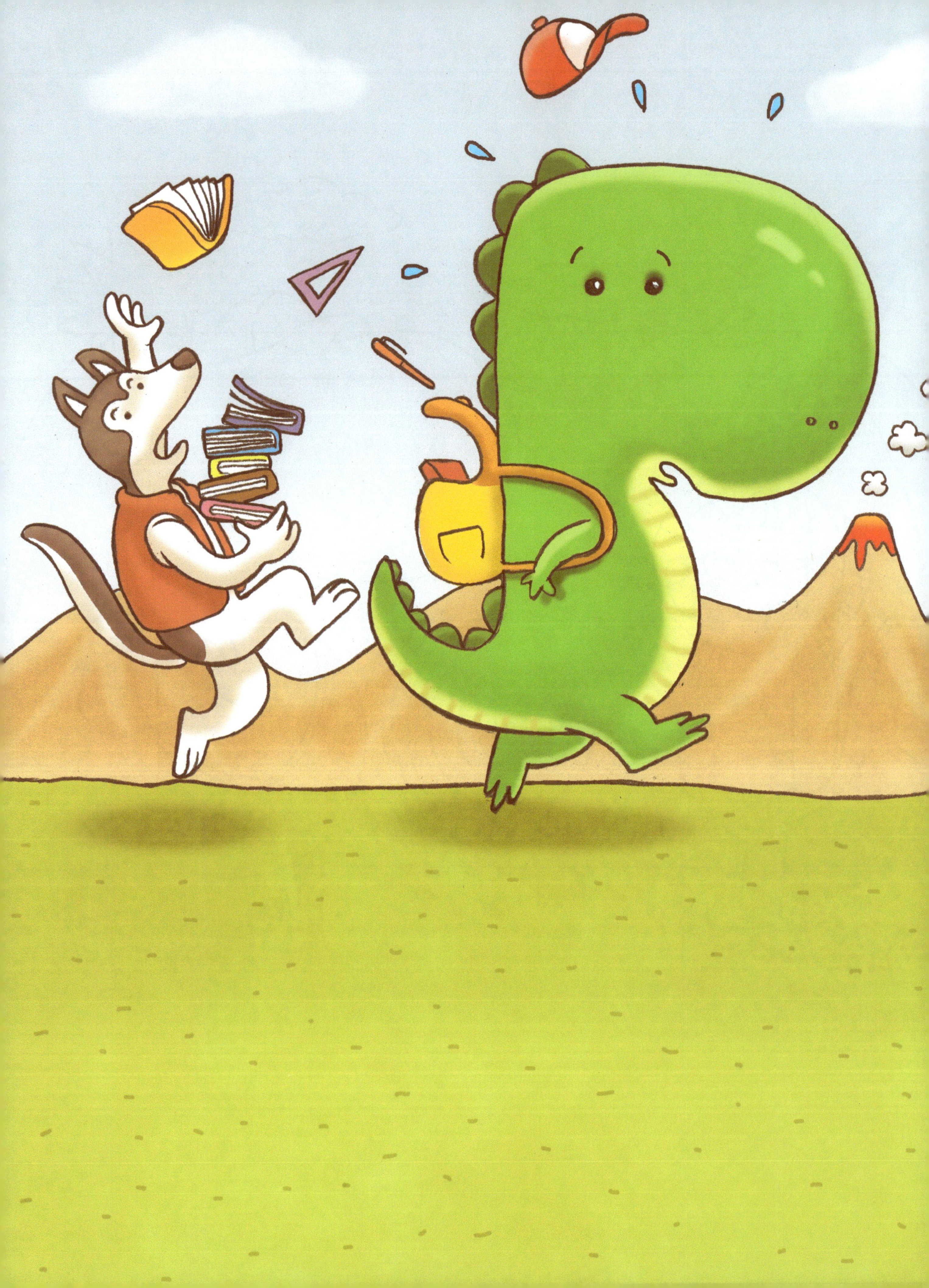

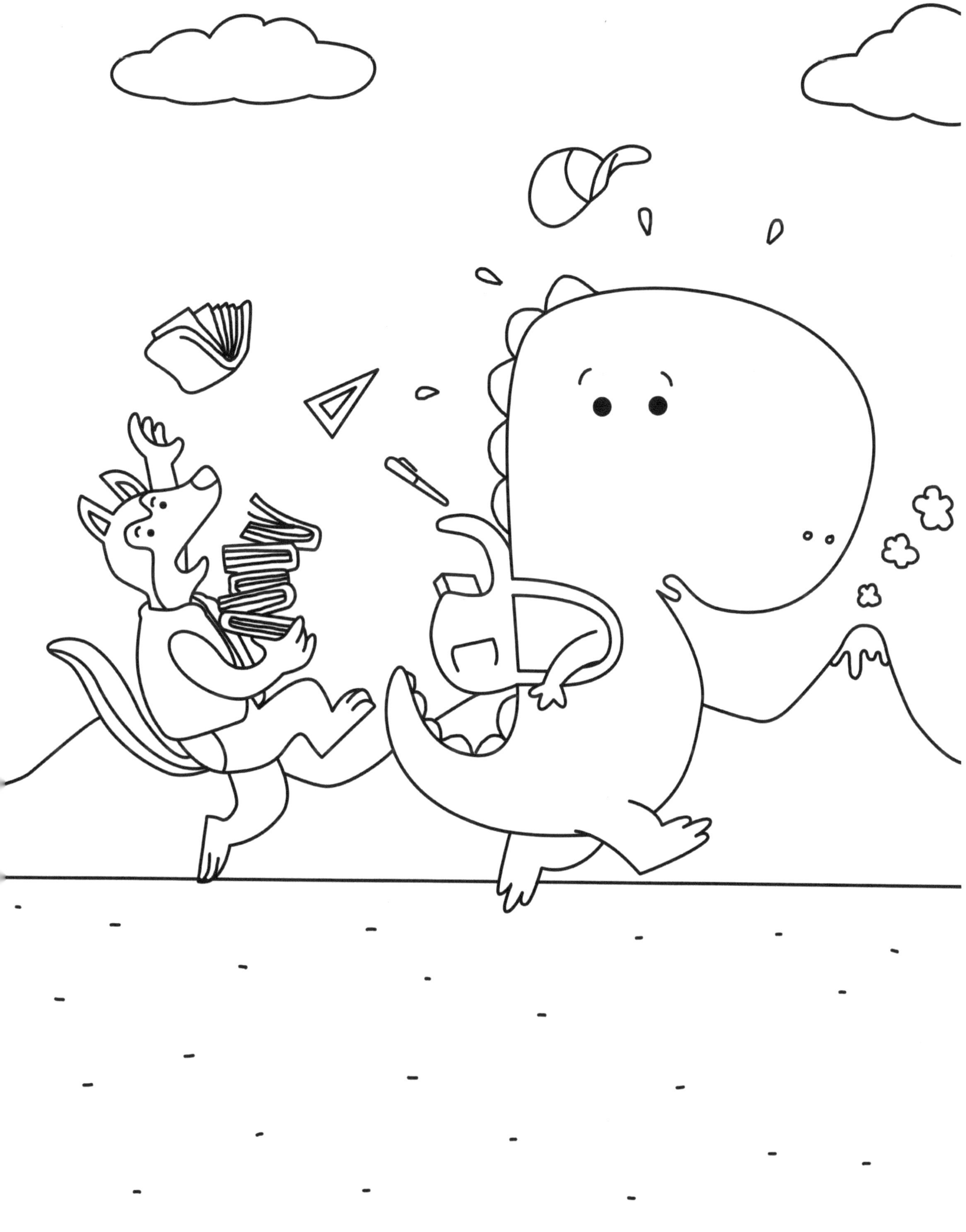

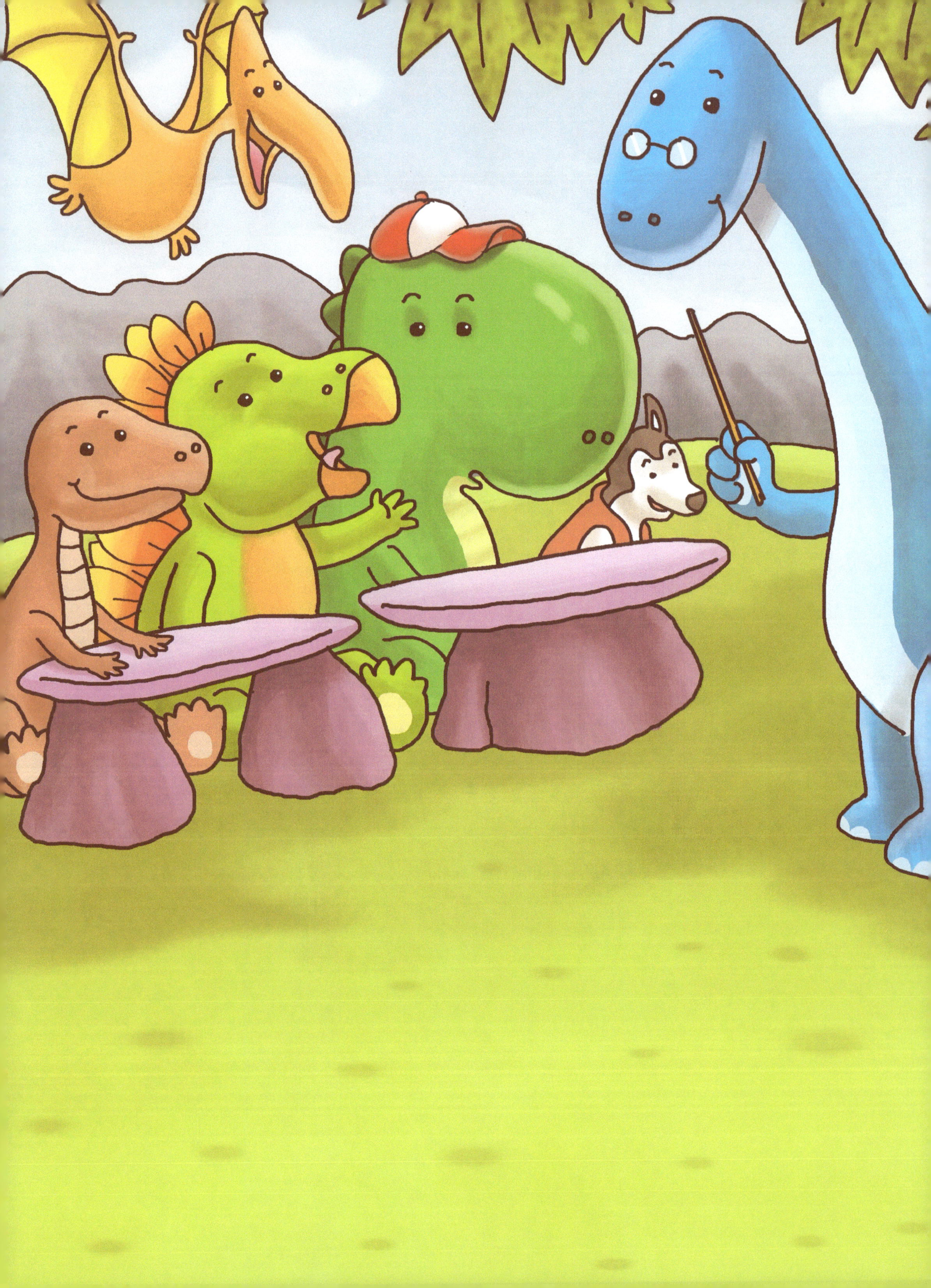

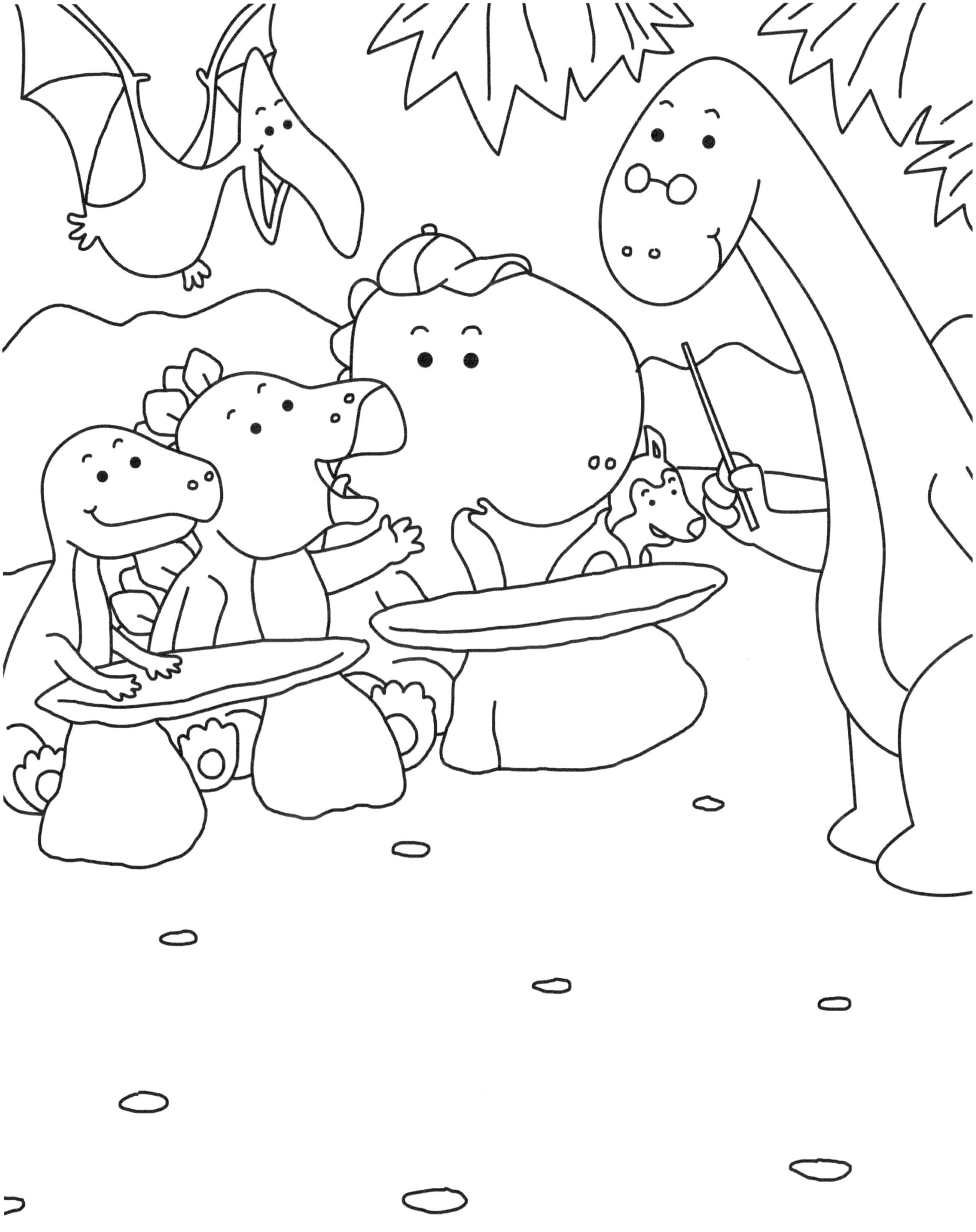

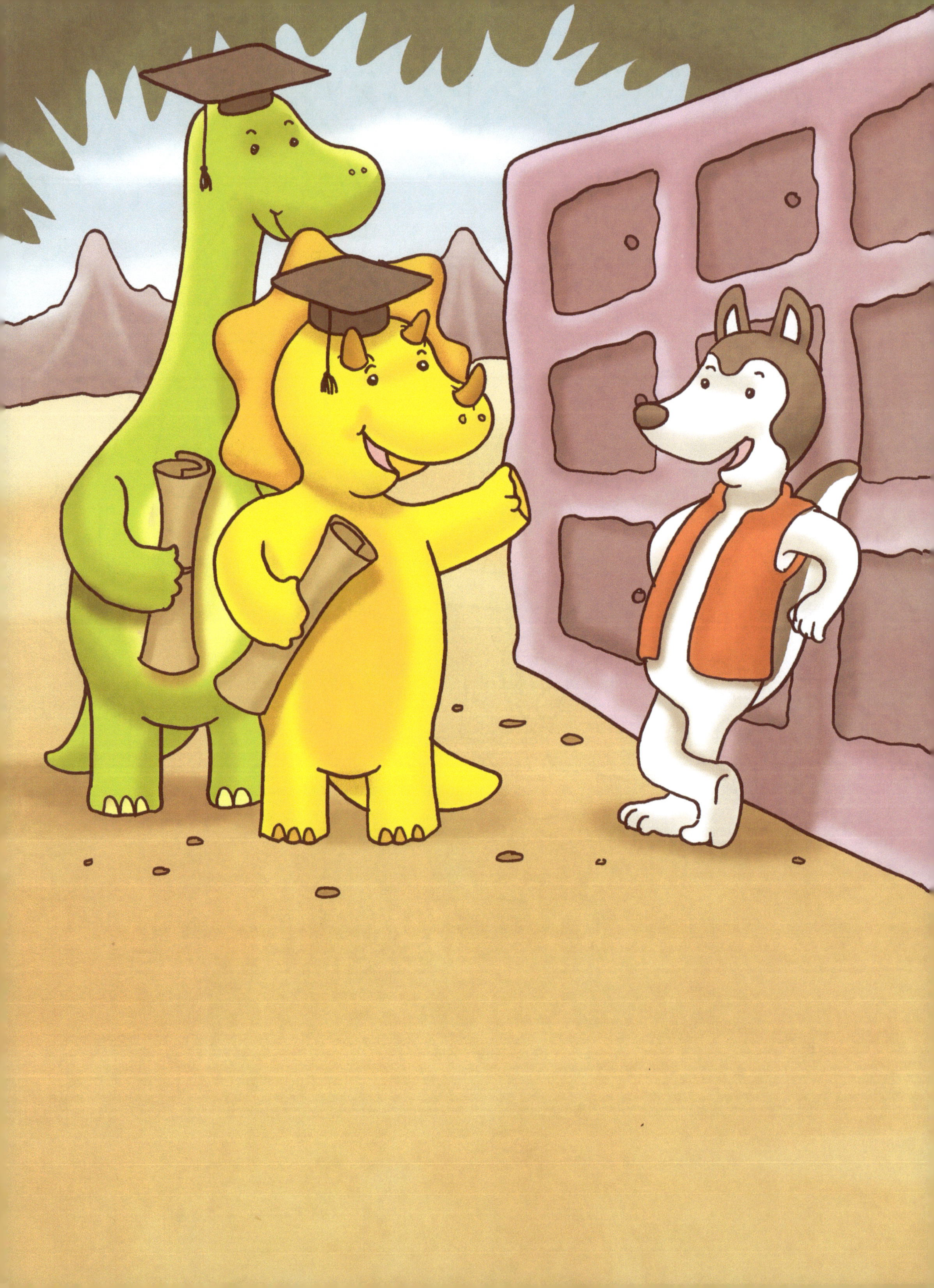

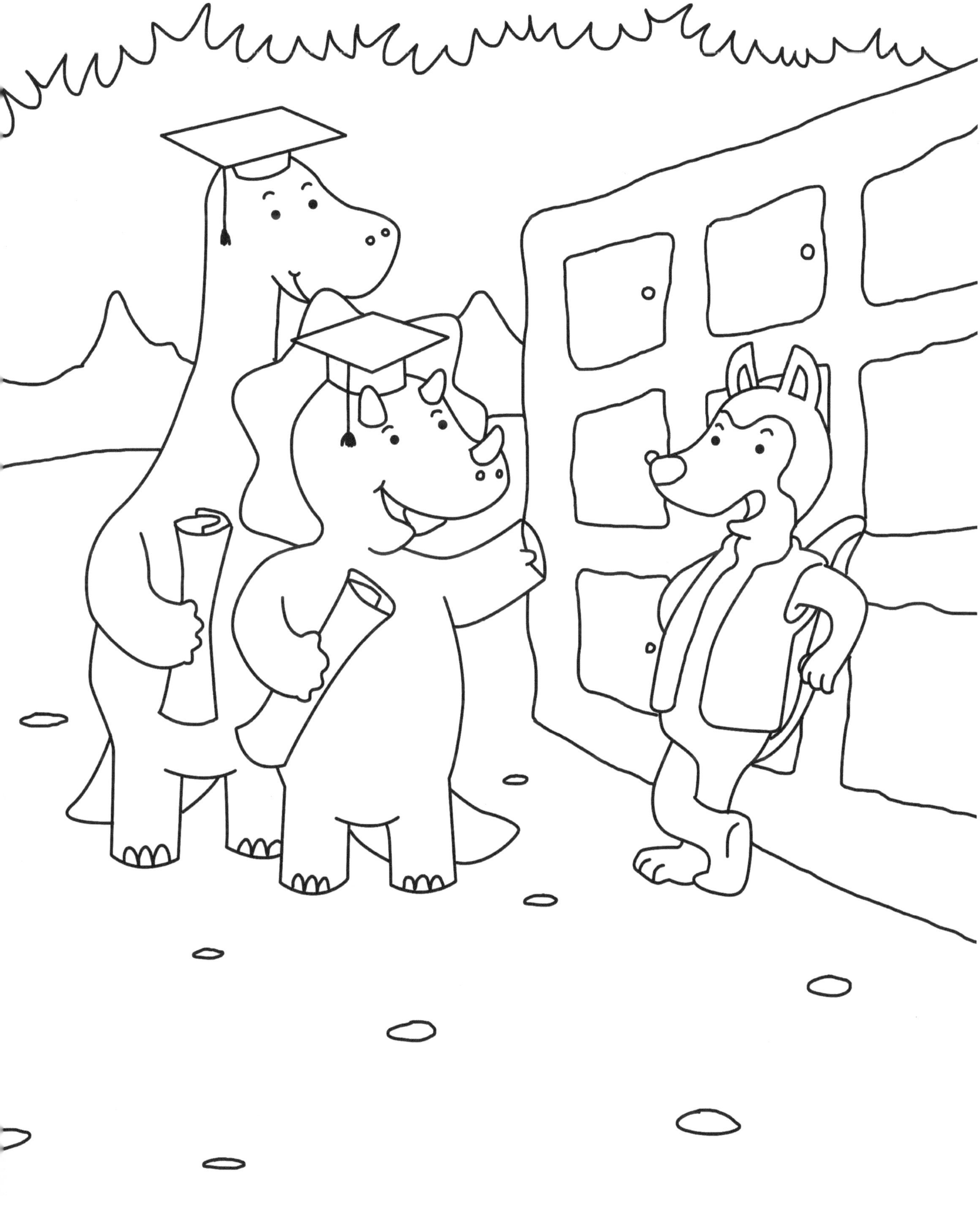

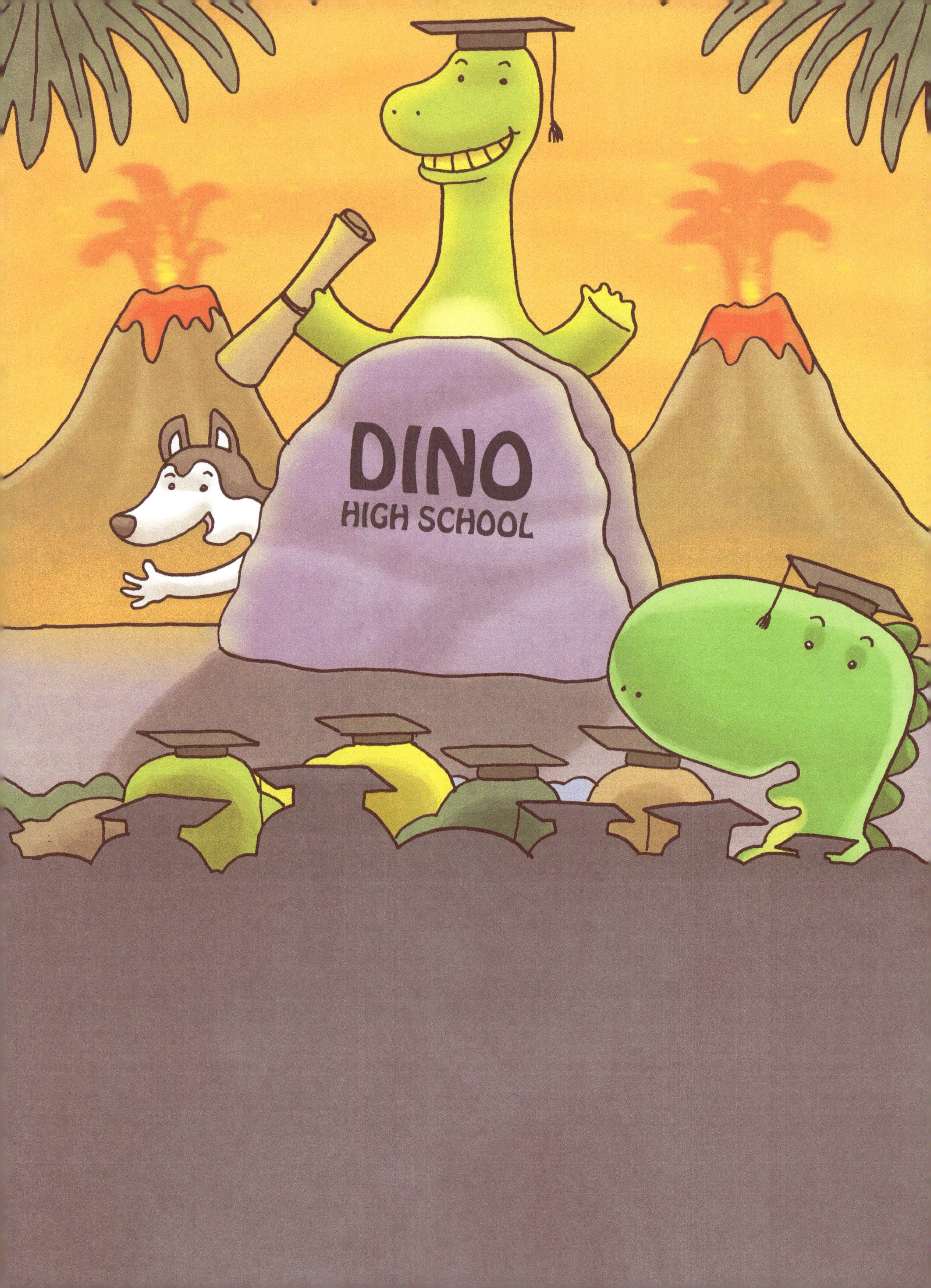
DINO
HIGH SCHOOL

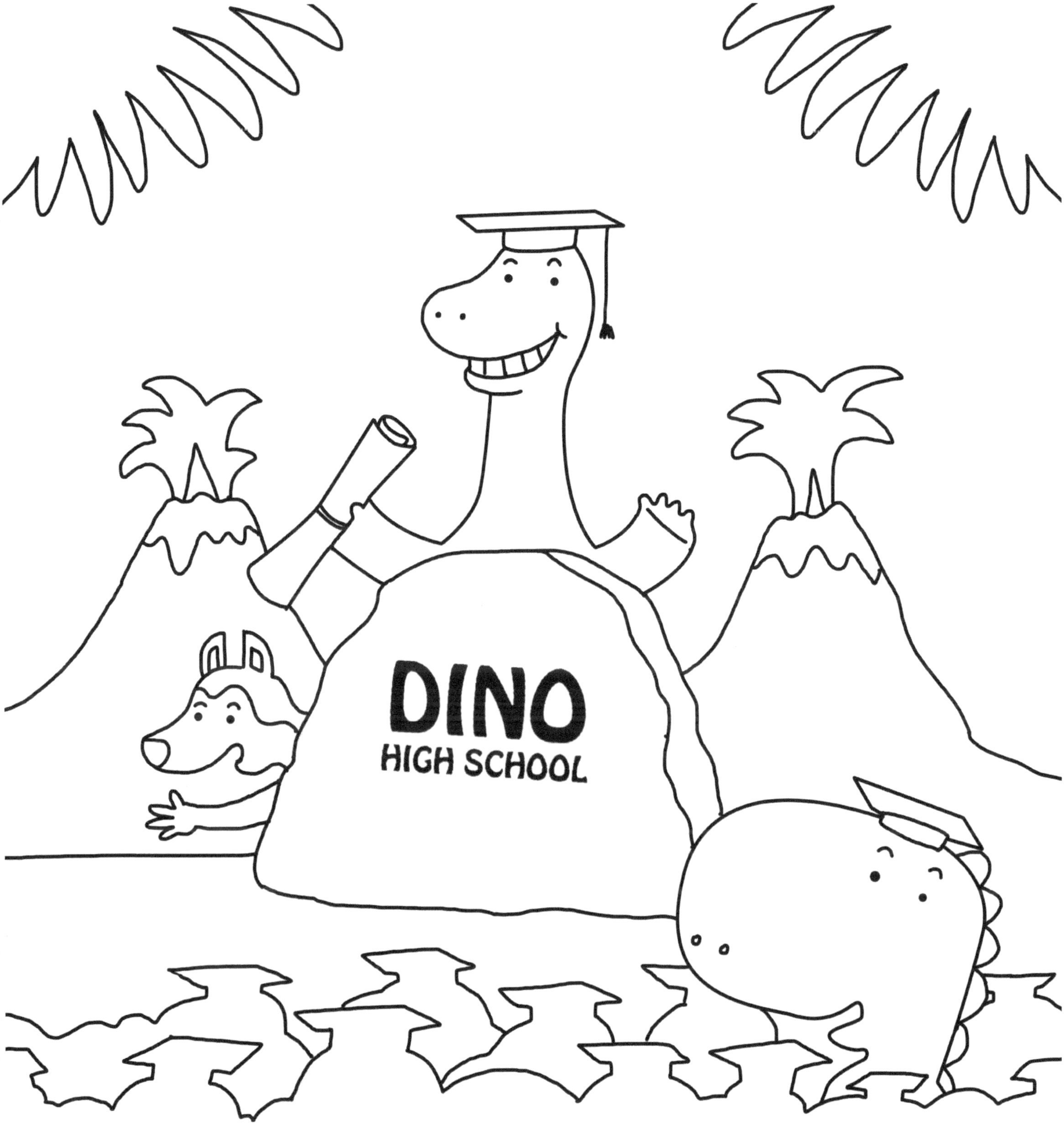
DINO
HIGH SCHOOL

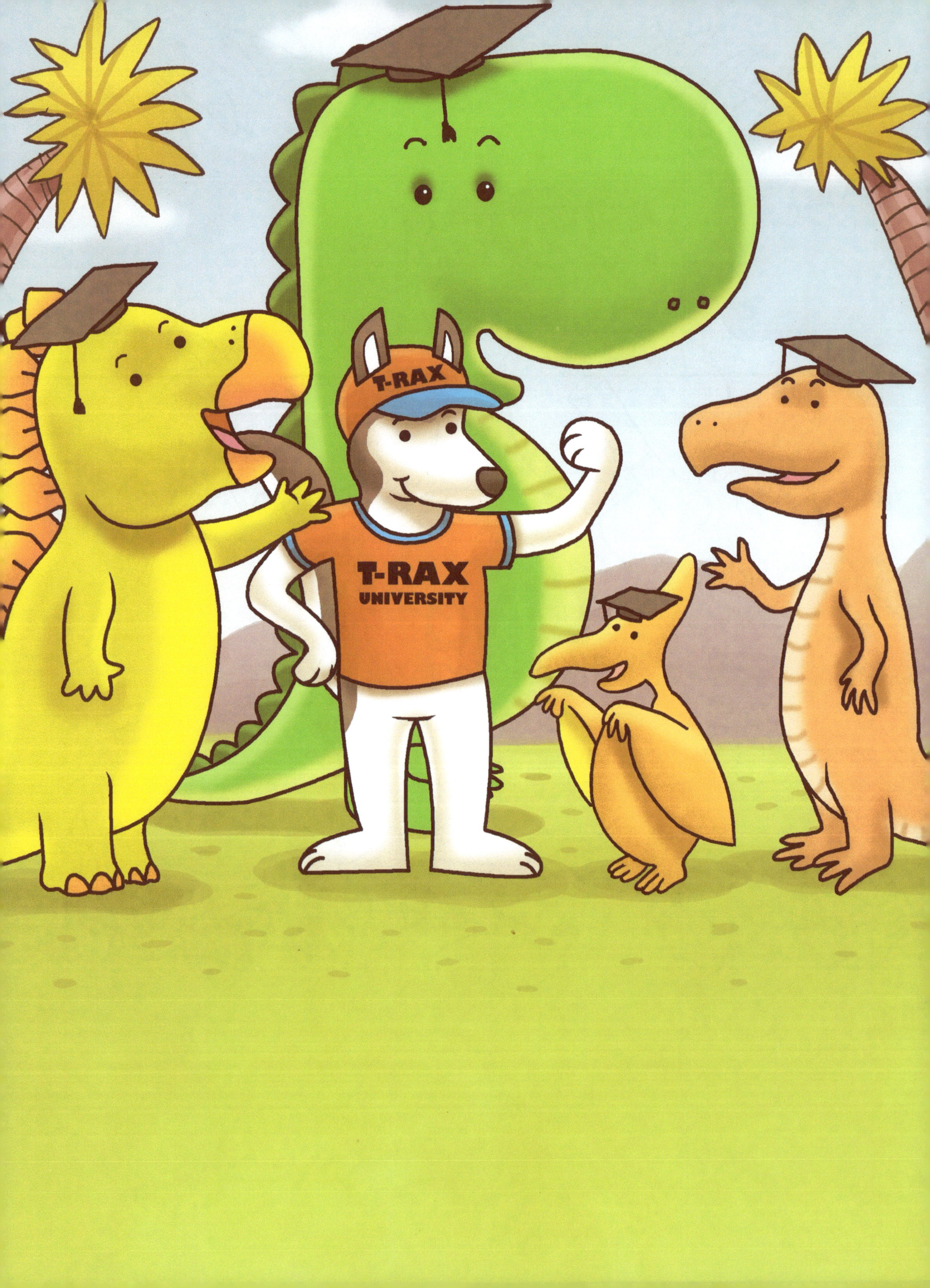
T-RAX
T-RAX
UNIVERSITY

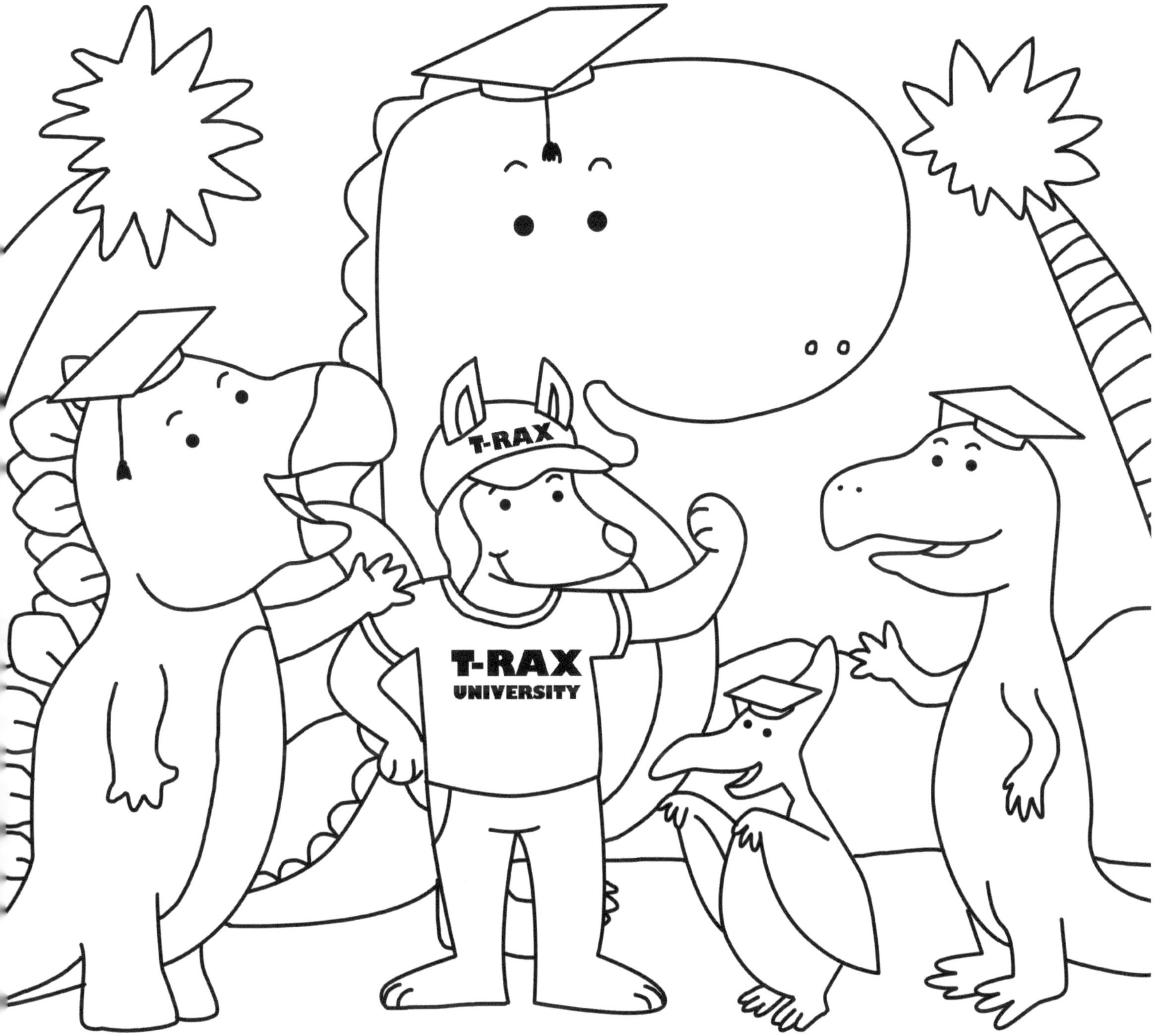
T-RAX
T-RAX
UNIVERSITY

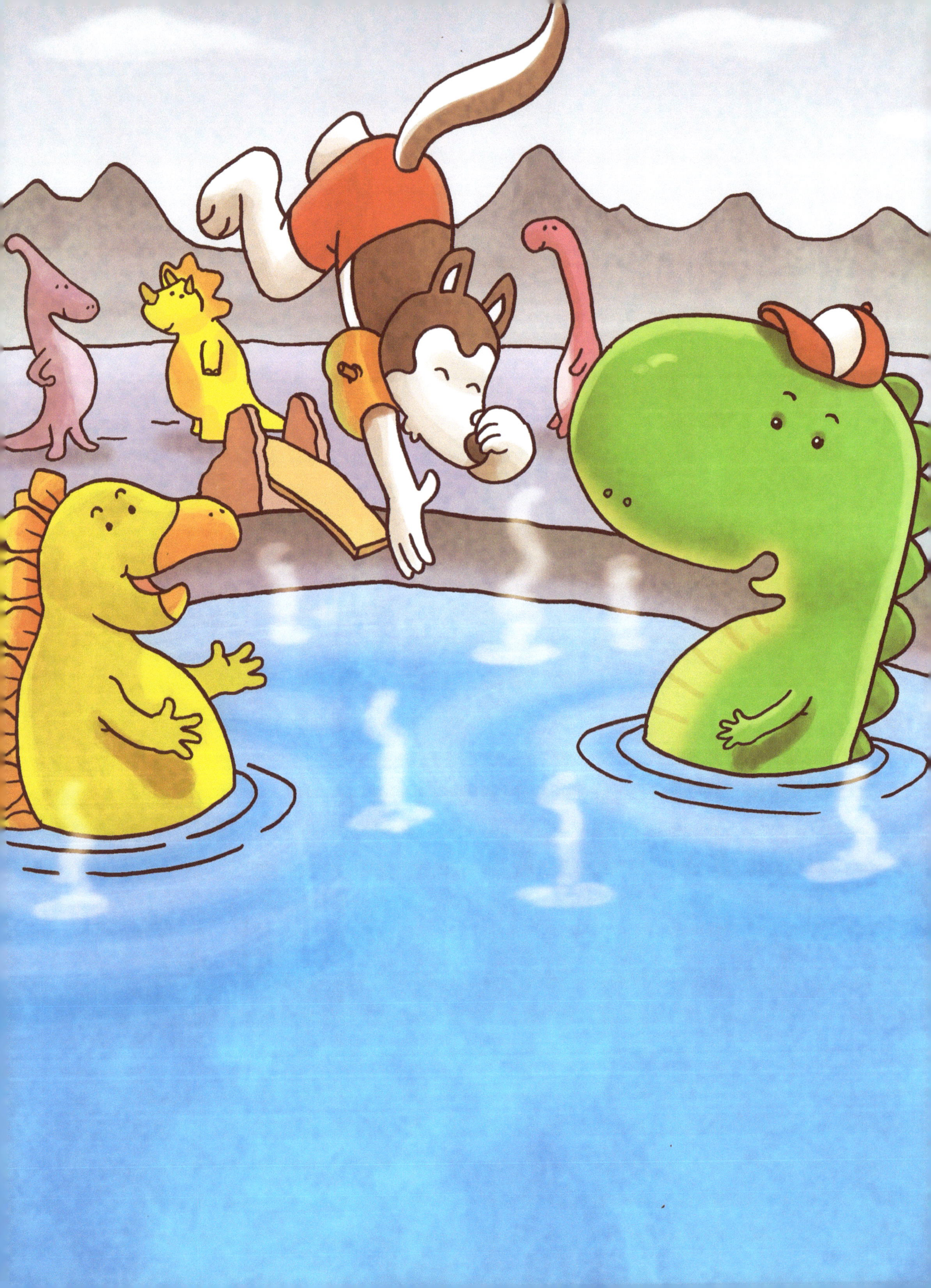

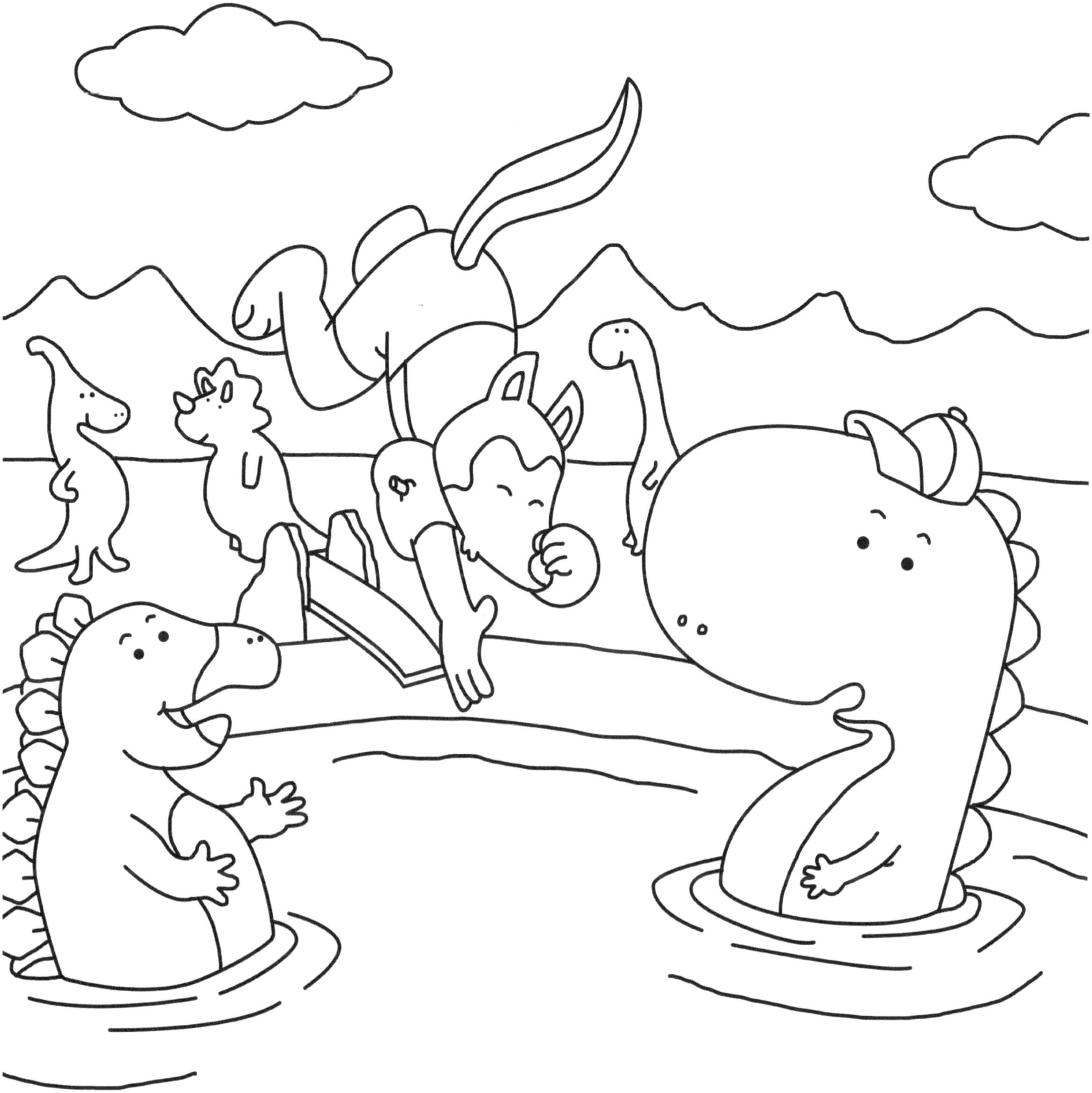

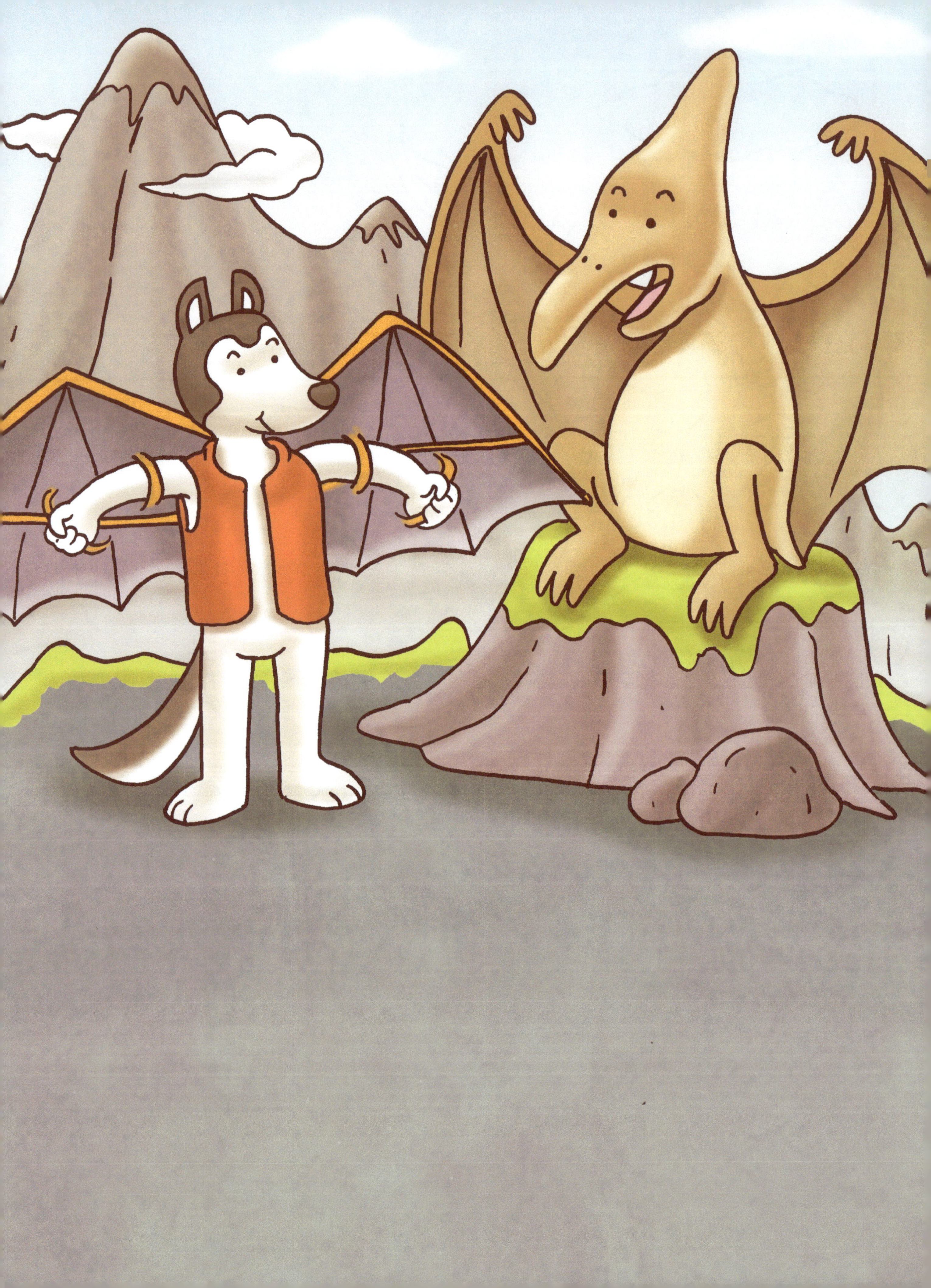

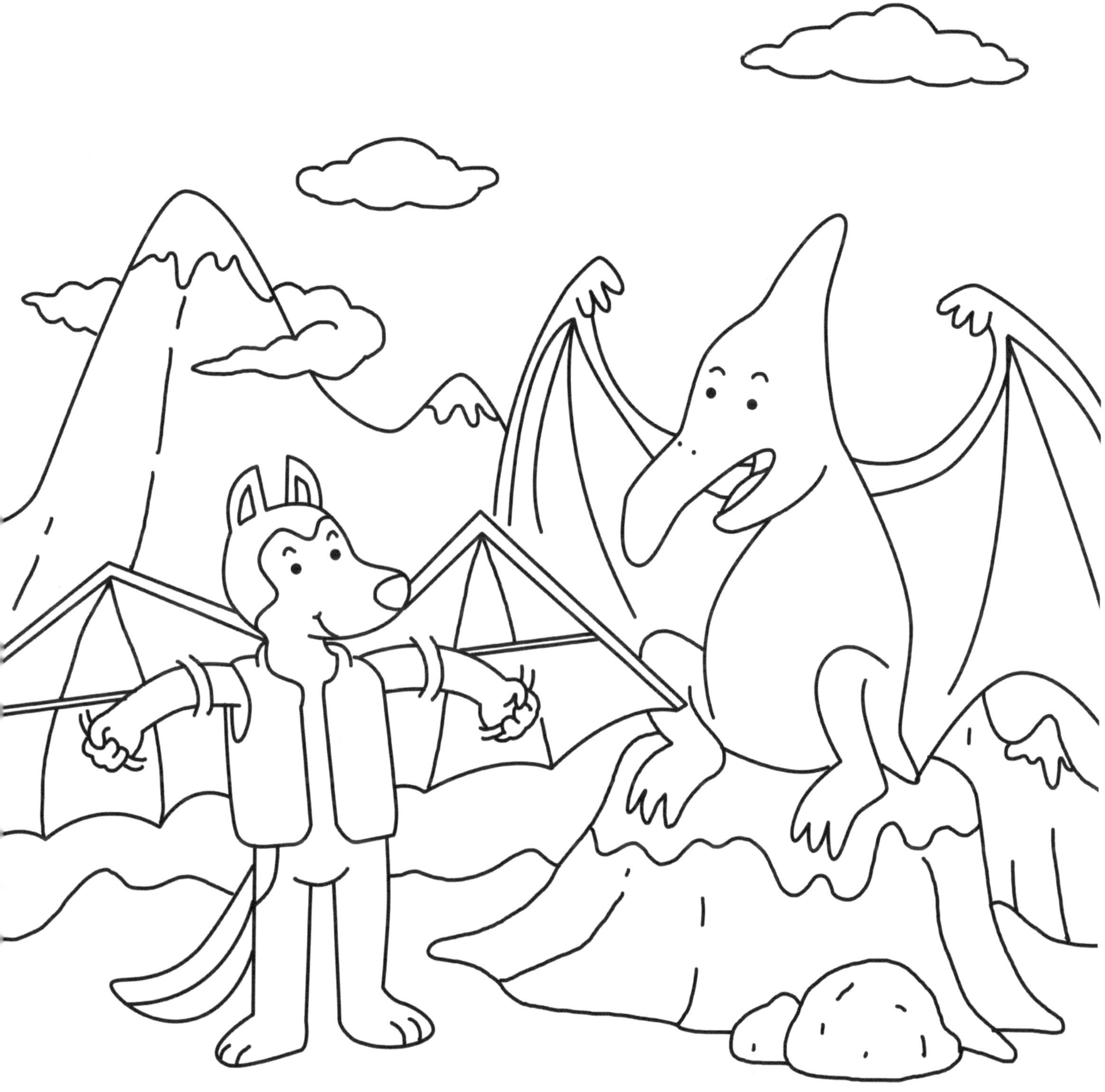

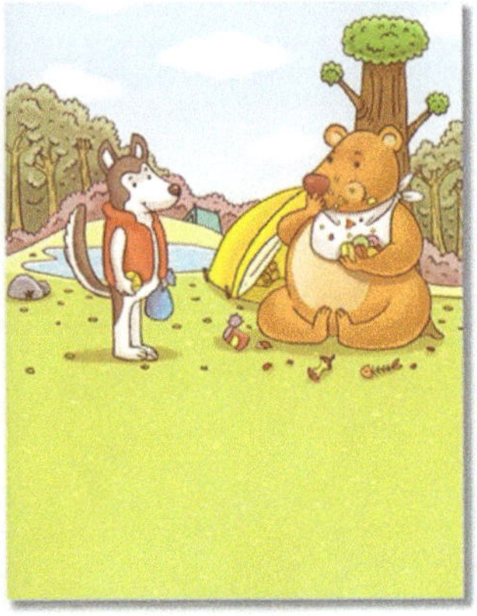
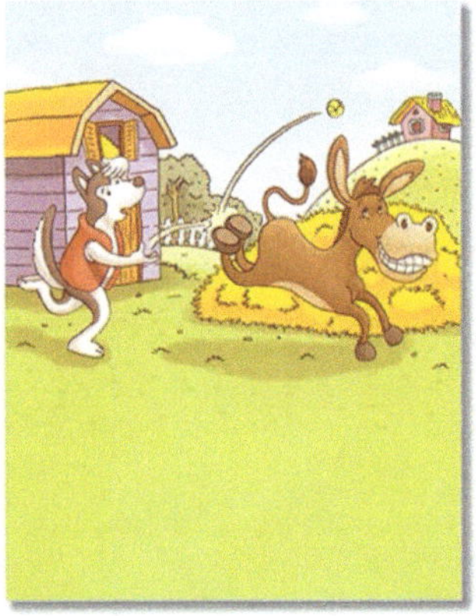
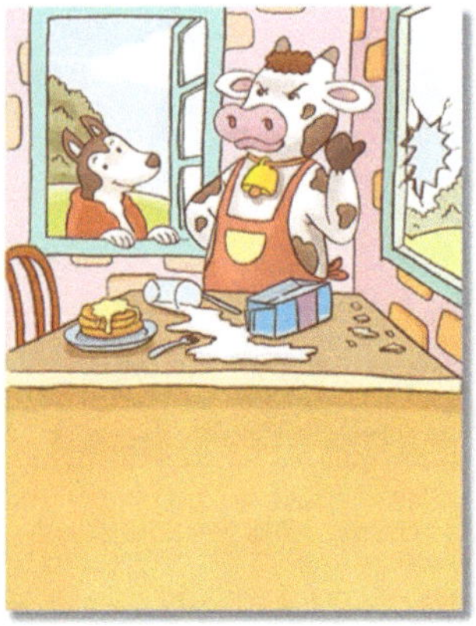
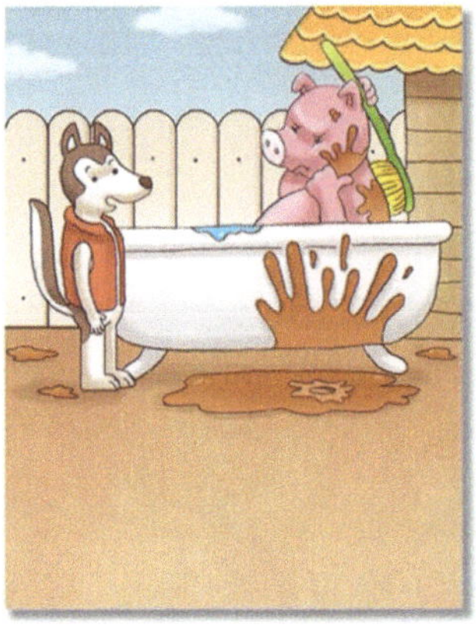
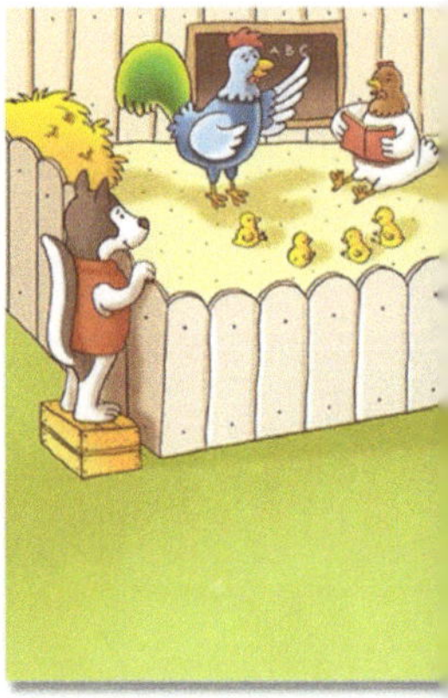
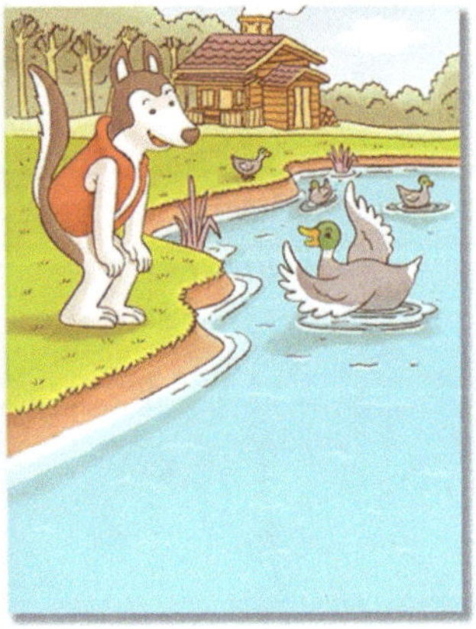
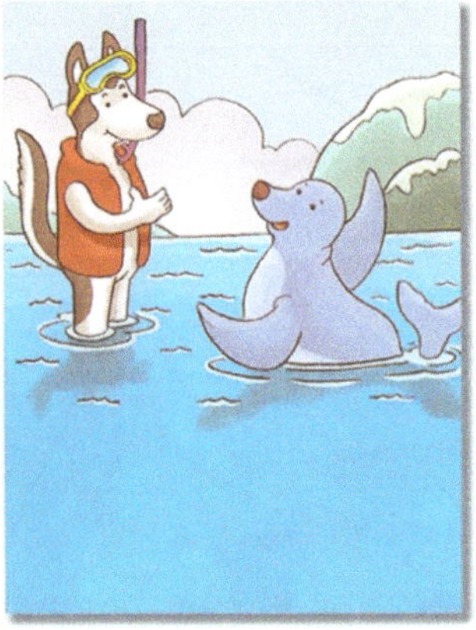
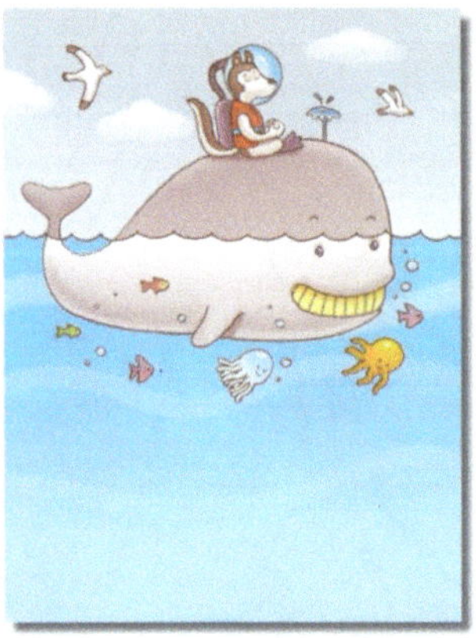
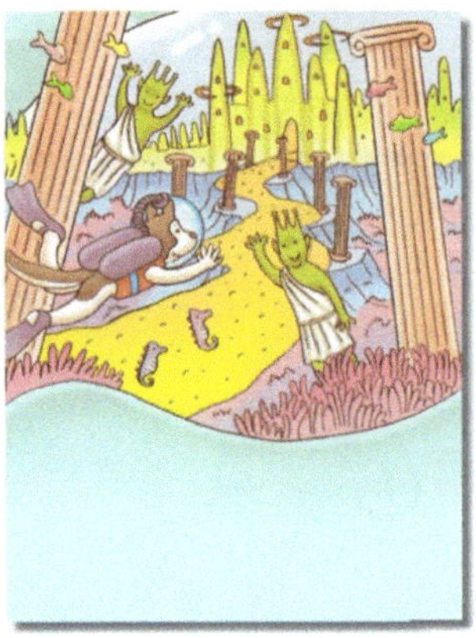
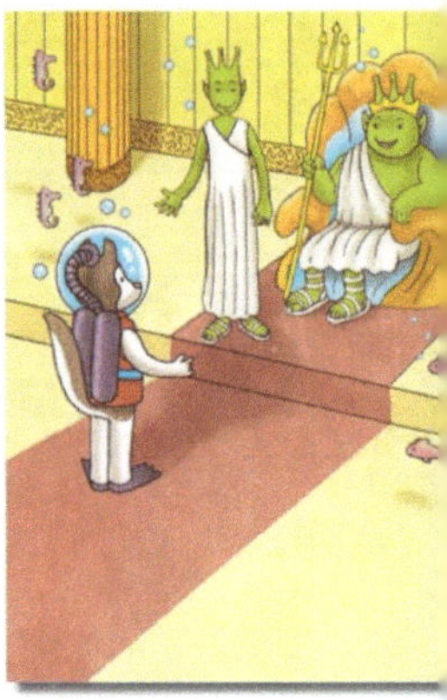
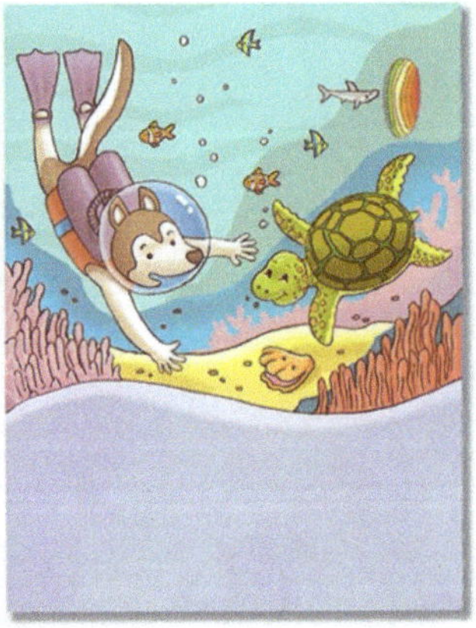
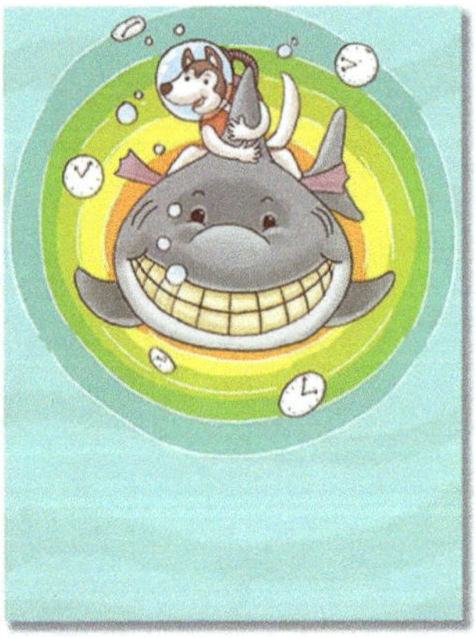
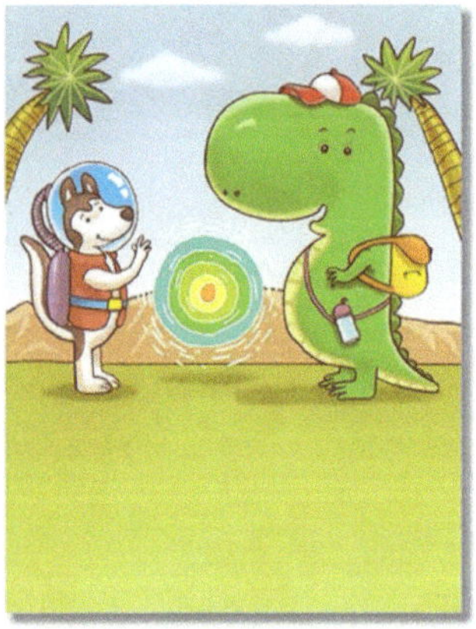
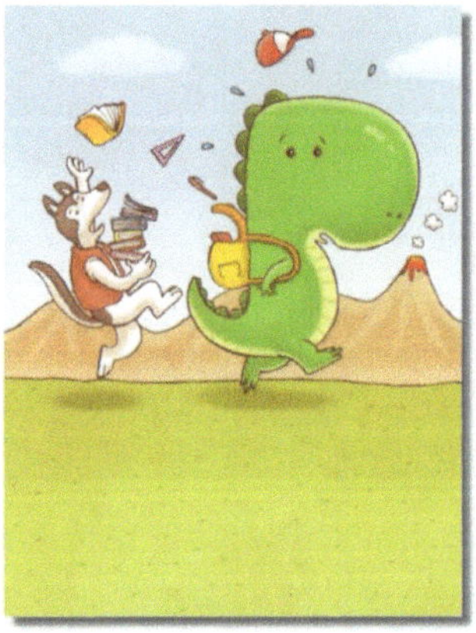
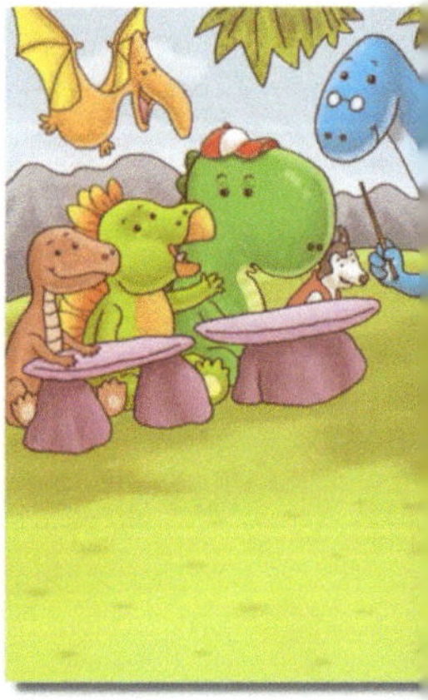
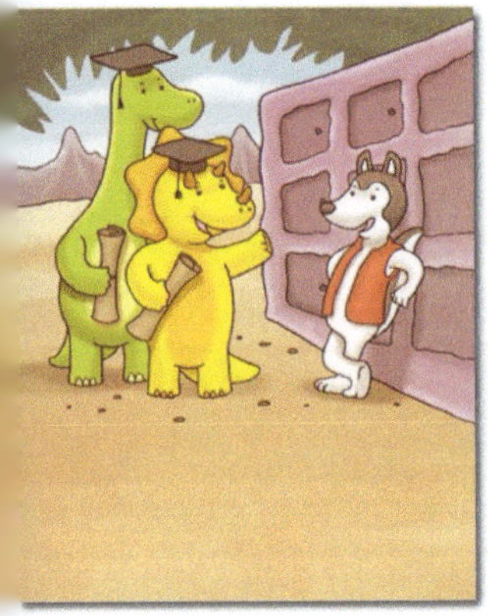
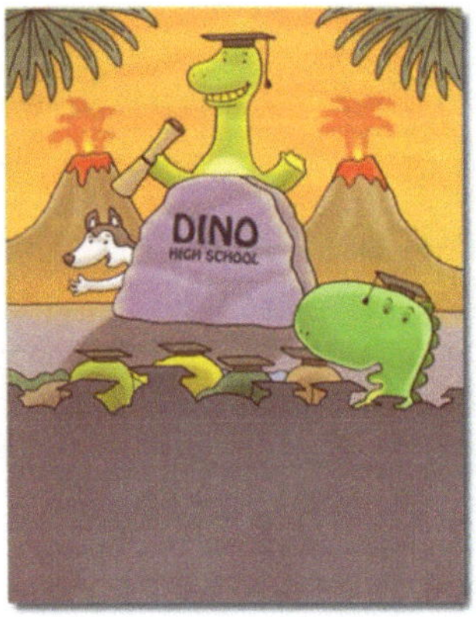
DINO
HIGH SCHOOL
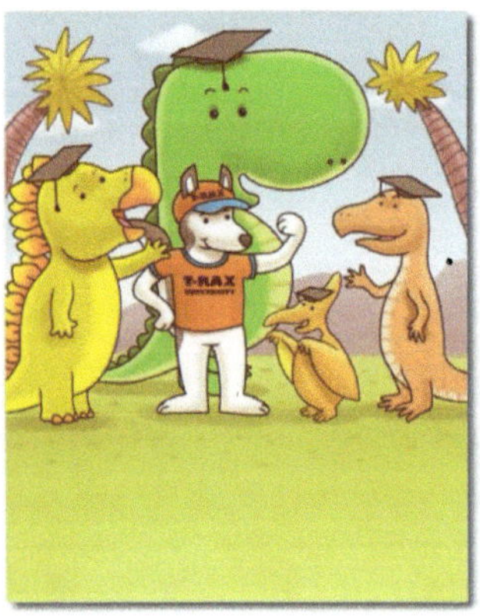
T-RAX
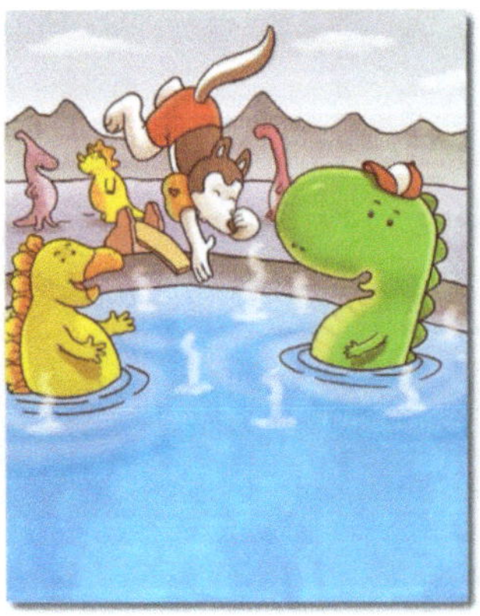
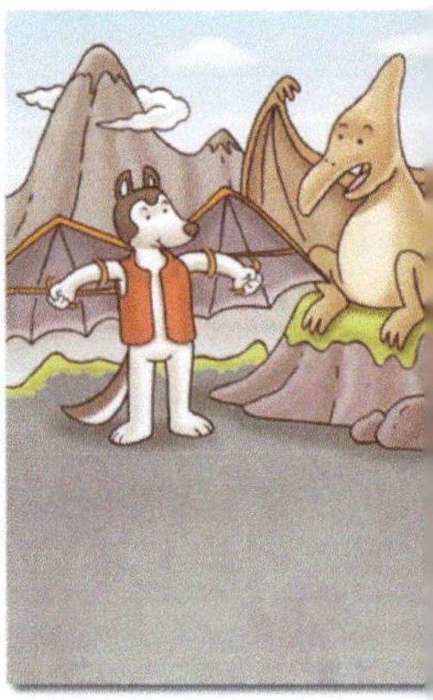

www.ingramcontent.com/pod-product-compliance
Lightning Source LLC
Chambersburg PA
CBHW051105180526
45172CB00002B/781
* 9 7 8 1 5 2 2 7 1 9 1 9 9 *